RESCUING

RUBY

Linny Lee Saunders

Silver Lake Publisher
3655 W. Anthem Way
Suite A 109, #305
Phoenix, AZ 85086

Linny's blog: PlaceCalledSimplicity.com

Book Website: RescuingRuby.com

Donations: InternationalVoiceoftheOrphan.com

To contact the author: aplacecalledsimplicity@yahoo.com

A portion of the author's royalties will be donated to "Ruby's Friends" @ *InternationalVoiceOfTheOrphan.com* Ruby's Friends was created to care for medical needs of orphans and special needs children in developing countries. Donations to care for orphans and vulnerable children can be made at **InternationalVoiceOfTheOrphan.com.**

Copyright 2015 by Linny Lee Saunders
All rights reserved
Printed in the Untied Sates of America
International Standard Book Number:
ISBN-13: 978-0692471968

Contents

DEDICATIONS

Above all else - dedicated to Almighty God. The true Rescuer of Ruby. You alone are worthy of all praise!

To my precious husband Dwight. God knew the dreams He had planted in my heart as a little girl for a huge family gathered tenderly from all over the world. No doubt, He also knew that not many men would be up for the challenge nor would many enthusiastically embrace it. You are the only man I know, who, at the age of 56, would passionately pursue bringing home a medically fragile one year old. I am so thankful for this life we've made together and the precious pile of treasures we've gathered {so far} over the last 37 years.

To our Emma - Your lifelong dedication to the broken bodied orphans of the world knows no bounds. Without your love and passion for "the least of these" there would have been no rescue of Ruby. Adults around were afraid of Ruby's fragile, emaciated and dying being, yet you Emma Joy gently and lovingly swooped in and began the ultimate rescue. We will forever be indebted to you for your sacrificial love for your baby sister. We are honored to call you daughter.

To Abigail and Ryan, Tyler and Sarah, Autumn and Karl, Emma and Josh, Graham and Savannah, Liberty, Jubilee, Nehemiah, Isaiah, Elizabeth and Elijah. Thank you for lovingly opening your hearts and showering Ruby with the joy of family - forever!

To my mom and dad - Thank you for praying fervently.

To thousands and thousands of blog friends around the world who have lovingly embraced and treasured our Ruby Grace from afar. There is no doubt, that your continual worldwide intercession on Ruby's behalf has played an integral part in her healing.

To Gordon and Deb, Kathi S., and Officer McC . Thank you each for your sincere dedication to helping us expedite Ruby's rescue.

To Dr. David Shafron - Ruby's beloved and highly skilled neurosurgeon. Your expertise has been Ruby's lifesaver and your gentle love for Ruby has blessed our family over and over.

To BA Captain Graeme S. who was used by God in a most miraculous way to help rescue Ruby. As well as **Jonathan** (the Cabin Crew Director) and **Sarah** of Flight 63, who both played an integral part.

To Stuart – You graciously and generously welcomed all of us, without hesitation, into your home for weeks and weeks! Your love for our pile of treasures is a beautiful thing. What a blessing you are, dear treasured friend!!

To my childhood friend Dave even though you live in Heaven, I have to believe that our sweet Father is whispering to you, "She finished it!" and you are celebrating from there. With tears, I regret you didn't get to read it before you suddenly left us. Thank you for cheering me on as I wrote! You are so missed!

To Dr. Pakhi of Colorado - You worked with diligence to find the right neurosurgeon to tend to Ruby. Thank you so very much!

To Artemis – Ruby's PT – You were Ruby's first 'friend' and I will never forget her wiggles of joy when you were coming to work with her! Thank you for teaching us how to help Ruby to become mobile.

To Lindsey - Ruby's caregiver and BFF – You have lovingly worked to help us unlock the hidden Ruby. We love you so much!

And saving the best for last - **to Ruby Grace** herself – your joyful, spunky, friend loving, sweet-spirited, God worshipping little being honors God with every breath! We are so grateful for you! To think, some thought you "would never do anything" - ha - such crazy talk!!

Your life, Ruby Grace, proudly displays the favor of God, His miraculous ways and His passionate love for the orphan! Oh how we love you sweet baby-girl! And we will never stop praising God that you were created and that you are ours - forever!

Introduction:

Sitting on the bed in Ruby's darkened Pediatric Intensive Care Unit on the 8th floor at Children's Hospital I begin. A story that must be told. A story that begs for hearts to be emblazoned for the orphan. A story that we have had the privilege of watching unfold: Ruby's story.

I once overheard someone say that it wasn't fair to use the word "rescue" when it comes to adoption. I completely understand what they were saying. And although each person's story is different, no doubt, once you have heard Ruby's story, you will have to agree, "rescue" is the only appropriate word when referring to bringing our precious littlest treasure home forever.

We are convinced that God spared Ruby's life over and over for a very specific purpose. And her story must be told.

RESCUING RUBY

Linny Lee Saunders

Chapter 1

In The Darkened Corner

It always amazes me how God works out each detail of our lives. It's true; He is always working the night shift on our behalf. He is orchestrating events behind the scenes so that we are in the right place at just the right time for His purposes. That is, if we are willing.

When my husband, Dwight, and our daughter, Emma, plan mission trips they plan around circumstances on the home front that need tending to. Family birthdays, weddings, upcoming surgeries, all must be figured into the mission equation. But the bottom line: Almighty God is the one who is maneuvering events to get each person where they need to be precisely when they need to be there, to accomplish His purposes and His plans.

So it was that Dwight and Emma were leading a team of twenty-two to minister to the orphans and hold a Legacy Leadership Conference for pastors and leaders in the summer of

2011. The plans were set into motion months before they actually departed for Africa in June 2011.

Not long after arriving in country, the team was up and headed to the orphanage where they had ministered often. It was the team's first day of service in Africa. Dwight and Emma had chosen to take the team to this particular orphanage first because it cares for 40 to 50 little ones from newborn to three years old.

After the introductory tour of the orphanage where expectations are shared, the team got to work feeding, changing, dressing and playing with the children. The team's purpose is to help the orphanage mamas anyway they can. With so many babies and toddlers the needs can be overwhelming to even the most seasoned parent!

Emma's heart tugged at her to begin caring for the babies. She had served here many times before and loved every minute of it. As Emma began to move about the cribs that day, she noticed a baby in a darkened corner. Moving closer, she gasped! Complete shock overtook her. She could not believe her eyes! She had never seen a baby look like this. Turning, she raced to find her dad.

Dwight looked up and saw Emma frantically running toward him, "Daddy come see this baby...she is dying!!" Following Emma to the darkened corner of the room, he was stunned at what he found, words inadequate to describe. Emaciated. Mere skin draped over her protruding bones. Her sweet head much larger than her boney exposed limbs. He gasped. 'Dying' is the only word that really could describe her. And at that divinely God-orchestrated moment, Almighty God broke his heart for her.

One baby girl, but a picture perfect representative of the millions and millions of orphans globally needing someone to desperately care about them.

Dwight called me immediately to say, "Linny, there is a baby here that is dying. She probably has Hydrocephalus, but she is dying." He started to cry, pleadingly he continued, "Ask for prayer on your blog.... beg people to pray for her.... she has to live Linny, she has to...I'm going to see what we can do for her.... please put it on your blog right now.... ask for people to pray for her.... her name at the orphanage is Rachel (name has been changed)." He went on to describe how this tiny little Rachel, who had completely stolen his heart, was unable to keep any formula down.

Our conversation was brief, but before we hung up, he again pleaded with me to put it on the blog immediately. I assured him that I would ask for prayer as soon as we hung up. I could hear the panic in his voice and I knew that I knew that God was doing something big at that very moment.

Emma emailed me a picture that night. She wanted me to understand. This was serious! This baby was going to die if people didn't pray!

I will never forget opening Emma's email attachment. Even though Dwight and Emma had described her, I was unprepared for her picture. Her eyes seemed to be pleading, "Will you help me? Will you love me? Will you rescue me?"

Her facial expression pleading, "Rescue me!"

And then I opened another picture:

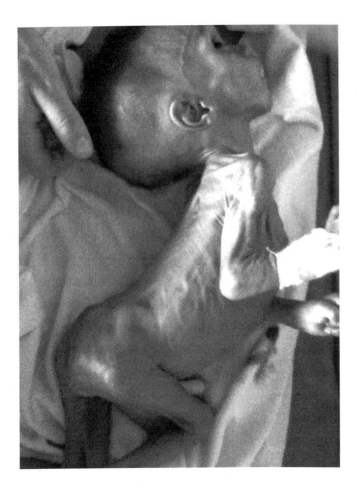

I gasped when I saw her emaciated being. Dwight had actually put His thumb up to her thigh and it matched in size. How can we comprehend the agony she had endured to this point?

Most orphanages have such great need, as there are many babies and very few caregivers. It's common for large holes to be cut in the bottle nipples to speed up the feedings. Large holes are needed to make the milky substance flow easily and quickly.

But baby Rachel could not swallow fast enough and the pressure in her brain from the likely Hydrocephalus was forcing her to throw up everything she was given. Despite the large bottles, she was still starving, completely unable to keep anything down.

I hurried to my laptop and wrote a blog post-urging people to pray for her, while trying my best to describe how desperate her situation was.

My blog friends, they just get it. They are passionate about the orphan and they know that prayer changes things. No doubt, most immediately slipped into 'intercession mode' for this little treasure.

I decided to ask blog friends to fast on Rachel's behalf as well. I could not think about this baby named Rachel without starting to cry. After posting the call to fast for her, many said they would join in.

When Dwight travels on international mission trips, he and I try to speak to each other a couple of times each day. There are too many circumstances on both home front and mission front that can be overwhelming. We find it helps in every way to touch base often.

14

After discovering Rachel, each conversation Dwight and I had began and ended with how Rachel was doing.

Dwight learned that she had only been brought to the baby orphanage about two weeks prior to Dwight and Emma's team arriving. A man walking in a garden had found Rachel abandoned, alone and dying. The man had lifted her out of the garden and taken her to the police station. The police in turn had brought her to the orphanage. She was estimated to be about a year old. She weighed just six pounds, and most of it was the water from the Hydrocephalus.

Dwight didn't know what to do with Rachel's constant vomiting. He knew he needed to find a way to keep food in her starving, gaunt and boney tiny being.

He talked to our oldest daughter, Abigail, who knew of a young woman, in a neighboring town in Africa, who was familiar with treating babies with Hydrocephalus and also with severe malnourishment. Abigail gave Dwight the number of her friend and Dwight was able to call and talk to her. It proved to be an invaluable call! The woman said, that assuming Rachel had Hydrocephalus, she definitely needed to be fed completely different than everyone else.

Hydrocephalus is a condition in which water remains on the brain unable to drain. Most born with Hydrocephalus in the western world have a shunt surgically inserted, which remains their entire life. Sometimes they will need to have a shunt replaced or fixed, but the shunt is in place to drain the fluid. If too much fluid builds up, a person will die.

Left untreated, the excess water in the brain produces constant pressure, which makes a little one vomit often. The tension between pressure in the head and excess food in the belly is a thin line...if Rachel was fed too much she would instantly vomit. Yet, because of the abuse she had suffered, she was in a state of severe starvation. The Hydrocephalus complicated this entire process, creating the need for Rachel to be fed tiny amounts frequently. A half-ounce every 15 minutes would be ideal.

Because she had been starving and was desperately hungry, she would gulp down several ounces at a time. But in the midst of the feeding, with still much of the bottle left, the pressure in her brain would cause her stomach to instantly throw up all she had just eaten.

Equipped with this new information from Abigail's friend, Dwight knew Rachel needed a completely different approach. Dwight began pleading for the caregivers to feed Rachel tiny amounts more often. Dwight also sought out any young volunteers serving at the orphanage. He would take them to meet Rachel and tell them, "She needs extra care! Please will you come and spend your time with just her? Will you do this for me and then pass on the message to the next person when you are leaving?"

16

This tag-team system among the volunteers was set up without any structure. Person after person was made aware of Rachel's desperate need for individualized care and each promised to pass the word along. "Feed this little treasure teeny-tiny amounts often. Love her. Sing to her. Pray over her. Tenderly spend all the time you can with her. She will die if she is not treated with extra special care. She's a miracle. Pass the word along when you are leaving."

We cannot possibly ever know all the people who would, over the next few months, spend time loving on our baby girl. We cannot possibly begin to show our gratitude to all those who took time out of their lives to serve in Africa and to specifically love her.

Each volunteer, whether a local resident or an international short-term missionary, who loved on our baby girl during this paramount time, is an integral part of her story. Their selfless love toward her was exactly what Jesus calls each of us to be: His hands and feet here on earth.

When I think of all the young people, many of whose names I do not know, whose faces we may never meet, yet each such an integral part of loving our girl, I am overcome with great emotion. Their sacrificial love that caused them to go to her crib in the corner, to scoop her out and whisper how much she was valued and loved, is beyond most people's scope of understanding. The reality that total strangers were loving her by feeding her tiny amounts of formula, gently changing her diaper, talking softly over her and without reservation, tears fall from my eyes. Their tender, selfless love for this dying baby girl is forever etched in our hearts and we can never thank them enough.

Each morning Dwight would have his Bible study, eat a quick breakfast, phone me, and then rush to check on Rachel. Choking back tears, he would end the phone calls with, "Please pray Linny that she is still alive when I get there." I tried to reassure him that I was praying, people around the world were praying and the Lord was listening. I didn't really have to tell him all that, but no doubt, her situation was desperate and he felt desperate!

After Dwight and Emma had found Rachel, they began to advocate for specialized medical care for her. Dwight went to see the Director and asked if he could take her to a local hospital for testing to see if, indeed, she had Hydrocephalus. The Director allowed him to take Rachel as long as a caregiver from the orphanage went along as well.

Dwight said it was extremely heart wrenching, agonizing and frustrating to watch them attempt to insert an IV in Rachel's arms.

Because of Rachel's severe malnutrition her veins had spread out in spider leg fashion. Her flesh was merely a cover draping her bones so there was nothing to cushion the needle at all

Alei was part of the **GO** team. She said it was so hard to leave
Africa wondering what would happen to her.

Baby Rachel wailed as they tried to insert the IV needle, but after several attempts, the technician just threw her hands up in the air and left. Rachel continued to wail and flail through the MRI. Dwight was sure that the pictures had to be blurry from the way she had thrashed about. It broke his heart and tears filled his eyes. He hated to see her suffering more obvious pain.

As the driver drove Rachel, Dwight and the caregiver back to the orphanage, Dwight cradled Rachel tight, singing to her the song he had already gently sung to her over and over and over,

"Oh how I love Jesus, Oh how I love Jesus, Oh how I love Jesus, because He first loved me. There is a name I love to hear, I love to sing its worth, it sounds like music to my ears, the sweetest name on earth, Oh how I love Jesus, Oh how I love Jesus, Oh how I love Jesus, because He first loved me."

After a few days of singing to Rachel the familiar song over and over, Dwight became convinced that her eyes began to lock onto his face. He even began to think that Rachel was beginning to understand that he was advocating for her.

In the days that followed, Dwight would hurry to the home as fast as he could to check on her, to cradle her and to feed her. Each time he was with her he would sing that same song over and over and over, *"Oh how I love Jesus."* It seemed to soothe her as he sang.

20

Dwight advocated for her care from any one willing to listen, continually asking the baby home mamas that Rachel be fed as often as possible.

A couple of days later the hospital report arrived for the Director confirming what everyone suspected. The diagnosis: Hydrocephalus.

Soon the days passed and before long Dwight and Emma and the team would head out of country. The rest of the team returning to the States, Dwight and Emma flying to a different west African country where he would again teach a Legacy Leadership Conference to pastors and leaders.

Dwight and I spoke about Baby Rachel. He was crying. I was crying. Who would advocate for her once he was gone? Who would fight for her to eat? Who would care?

It is a staggering thought that there are millions of orphans worldwide. Truly, the numbers are mind-boggling. Yet, in the enormity of the numbers, it really just boils down to one.

One that each of us can fight for.

One that each of us can advocate for.

One that we can each make a difference for.

Just one!

Daddy's been singing to her, "Oh how I love Jesus".

As Dwight prepared to leave he went to talk to the Director three separate times. Each time he told her, "Linny and I are willing to do anything for Baby Rachel. Anything. Anything at all. Please do not let money stand in the way of her care. Whatever she needs, we will pay for. We will do anything for her. Anything." Three times he told the Director this. We wanted to be sure she understood. Anything. Anything. Anything.

****

Dwight and Emma flew on to the next country and we had no way of being updated on Rachel's condition. We fasted, we prayed and we waited. They were ministering in the next country for almost a week.

Each day all I could think about was baby Rachel. I began to pray that God would allow her to come home to us. It was a long shot. We had heard that the Director was not exactly excited with the prospect of large families and we weren't exactly young. But it never hurts to pray!

In fact we have long said, "Ask any orphan if they would rather have old parents or no parents and we're pretty certain, hands down, that they would pick the oldies."

What was kind of crazy was that just a month earlier I had been talking to a friend on the phone. Something was said about bringing home a baby. I had rather nonchalantly quipped, "Well if anyone approached us about a baby we would decline. There are lots of young folks out there to care for the babies."

The Lord must have been chuckling when He heard that come out of my mouth and thinking, "Wait till you see what I have in store for you, Linny Lee, in just a few short weeks." Who would have thought about three weeks later I would be begging God to allow this teeny-tiny sweet baby girl to come home to us?

The week passed slowly and Dwight and Emma were soon headed back to the States. To our shock, when Dwight and Emma landed in Chicago on their way home, Dwight found an email awaiting him in his inbox from the Director of the baby home. It read {in part}:

June 22, 2011

"Pastor Dwight:

Just wanted to give you an update on Rachel.

When we took back the results to Dr. B, his report was very disappointing and I do not want to believe it. He said that from the scan, it shows that in addition to the water in her head, Rachel's brain has not properly developed like a normal child and that there is nothing that can be done for her. He also said that taking her to CURE hospital in Uganda would not help! I will however believe the report of the Lord that Rachel will be well. Will you believe this with me?

We then saw the pediatrician in the city hospital - who happens to be on the Orphanage Board, and she thinks that if we can first treat the malnutrition and when she has gained weight, we can then take her to CURE Hospital.

Pastor Dwight, in our last conversation with you before you left you mentioned that you would do anything to see that Rachel makes it. This is a private and confidential question: Would you consider adopting her so that she can get whatever treatment she needs from America and a good family as well? Just be honest and tell me what is on your heart. It is okay if you said no.

Thank you so much for the support your group gave to our orphanage during the two weeks you were here."

Dwight phoned me from the airport and questioned, "Did you get the forward?" I had not, so he briefly told me what it said as I ran to my computer to read it for myself. As I read, I began to weep. "Oh Whitey, this is exactly what I have been praying...."

Our words bubbled over. We were both clearly smitten with this frail little treasure!! Could it be that God really would allow us this unforeseen privilege? I could not stop bawling with humble joy!!

Later that day I drove with the kids the four hours to Albuquerque to pick up Dwight and Emma at the airport. We needed to talk and we needed to talk fast!

Little did we understand that saying, "YES" to Rachel would forever alter our family, our hearts, our home's geographic location and our 20 plus year occupation. But God knew. He was orchestrating monumental events, forever changing the trajectory of our lives and bringing us a rare privilege for which we would be eternally grateful!!

As I mentioned earlier, we had not been on a baby path. We had not been in pursuit of a little one needing 24/7/365 care, but when God moves on hearts to the point where we are pleading, "Pick me! Pick me! Pick me!", we can rest assured, it is definitely Almighty God moving!

The older I get, the more convinced I am that when we are presented with an opportunity that comes out of nowhere, has not been sought after and could only be used to bring Him glory, we are certainly on the right track to finding His perfect will!

We opted to Skype the Director and tell her so we both could hear her response. Her reaction was a blessing - she was joyous! We told her to please give baby Rachel a hug and kiss and tell her that her mommy and daddy would be coming for her as fast as we could get there!

The adventure had hardly begun - it was time to kick into gear and get our home study update completed so we could get our little gem home as quickly as possible!

Chapter 2

Eight Minutes

Immediately we were in the throes of updating our home study and filling out immigration paperwork. We also knew we needed to choose a name for this sweet bundle. We prayed. We take naming our children very seriously. We always weigh several factors including what the name means and what it will mean when spoken over our little one for their lifetime.

With such a traumatic start to her life, we needed a name that would convey God's plans for her. We narrowed our name search down. While investigating the name 'Ruby', we found that a flawless ruby is actually of more value than a diamond.

We decided that each time we spoke her name, we were placing God's infinite value over her and we would tell anyone that would listen that she was named Ruby, "because we believe she is a precious gem from the very heart of God."

Our home study was just about finished when, suddenly, on Sunday, July 17th, our daughter Autumn's boyfriend, on his way to pick Autumn up for church, was in a near-fatal motorcycle accident. Those tending to Karl did not know if he was going to live. Karl was taken by med flight twice, underwent emergency brain surgery and now lay in a coma with a traumatic brain injury (TBI). Life as we knew it screeched to a horrifying halt.

We were beyond distraught. We loved Karl, we loved his parents and we loved our daughter. Autumn had lost her first love in a tragic car accident on a sunny Sunday in July a few years earlier. Karl's accident was all too reminiscent of that horrible season in our lives just a few years before. There was no way I could leave Autumn alone. She refused to leave the ICU for weeks and we would not leave her side. She was much too fragile, especially after already enduring the loss of her first love.

For the first few days we stayed in the city that Karl had been taken by med flight to. It was about an hour and 20 minutes from our home. His TBI was extremely serious and they were not sure he was going to make it at all. With the first 48 hours touch and go, we had to be close to Autumn.

After the first 48 hours, we were able to go home, but still each day we drove the hour and 20 minutes to the ICU waiting room to sit with her. We wanted to be with her and we also wanted to minister to Karl's family. This unforeseen situation left little time to finish up the necessary paperwork that needed to get done to bring Ruby home. We drove home emotionally exhausted at night in time to make dinner and get the kids to bed.

While sitting in the ICU waiting room one day, I shared with Karl's Aunt Lisa my heartache about the holding pattern to get Ruby home. Without a moment of hesitation, Lisa wisely responded, "Linny, you be about God's business and God will be about your business."

Hmmm. I'd not heard that saying before, but it resonated with my heart. Lisa was insistent that God would move mightily on Ruby's behalf as we ministered to Karl's family, those around us whose loved ones were also in the ICU and to our own Autumn.

After 15 days in a coma, miraculously, Karl began to wake and there was talk of him being transferred to the Rehabilitative Hospital in Denver. At about the exact same time we received an email from the Director of Ruby's orphanage. "She is not doing well. The infection in her brain is there and her head is larger. Can you come quickly? She needs you."

Oh my goodness.

Our home study was just about done, but now it all needed to go to Immigration for approval before the African side would even entertain the thought of us bringing Ruby home. Little did we know that Almighty God was already moving enormous mountains behind the scenes. He was indeed 'going about our business' as we had been about His, just as Lisa had mentioned.

While we had been at the hospital day and night, Kathi at Chinese Children (the adoption agency doing our home study) was praying and working and remembered an Immigration officer that she had worked with before. She emailed her and asked her to help. Then she phoned her. Kathi, unbeknownst to us, was taking up the fight for Ruby Grace!

At the same time, our 7th child, Jubilee, had yet another terrible ear infection. Jubilee Promise had come home to us from China when she was eight years old. She has an extremely rare chromosomal syndrome that does not even have a name - it is that rare! As of 1999 there were only 50 known people in the world who have this rare chromosomal anomaly.

Jubilee had been plagued with so many ear infections that our pediatrician had decided to send her to Denver for testing. As soon as Karl was out of ICU, pending his transfer to a rehab in Denver, Jubilee's pediatrician had made an appointment for her in Denver for extensive testing.

About the same time, Kathi at our home study agency was able to speak to the Immigration officer who agreed to look at Ruby's picture if Kathi would email it to her. The picture of Ruby is a powerful picture. Barely six pounds and over a year old!

When the immigration officer saw Ruby's picture she responded quickly, "They have an immediate invitation to come and get fingerprinted."

Each previous international adoption we had done, we had to fill out an application, send a large check and wait for the US Immigration office to process the request in order to even get an invitation to come and be fingerprinted at an Immigration Office. Although there is nothing complicated about the process, it would take far more time than a very medically fragile Ruby could wait.

We learned from Kathi that the average wait for Immigration Approval to adopt from a foreign non-Hague country was running, at the time, about 75 days. Which means that after you are fingerprinted, one still has to wait an average of 75 days to get US Immigration clearance. Of course, from application to invitation for fingerprinting also takes weeks, which must also be added to the 75 days. This could be a total of almost three months for the US to send the document saying Ruby has permission to enter the United States.

Ruby didn't have 75 days to wait for approval!! Yet God was indeed "being about our business" as He moved on Kathi's heart to take up Ruby's cause, which stirred a loving Immigration officer's heart to move with record speed on Ruby's behalf.

As God in His perfect plan would have it, the girls and I were in Denver for Jubilee's testing and had spent the night in a hotel near the hospital since Jubilee's tests had not finished until late in the day.

Early the next morning, completely out of the blue, my cell phone rang. I thought it odd that our friend and pediatrician, Dr. Pakhi, would call so early!

When I heard her voice, I knew instantly something was wrong. Dr. Pakhi is a tenderhearted, gentle, loving professional, who truly cares about her patients. We were so blessed to have her caring for our children.

Dr. Pakhi asked if any doctors from Denver Children's had phoned me yet. I was perplexed. No, I had not had any calls, besides it was still very early in the morning. She continued. The tests had revealed a rare, yet potentially serious problem and Jubilee would need immediate surgery. There was concern that the growth spotted had already penetrated the lining of the brain. I was stunned.

Just days before Karl had just been moved to a Denver rehab hospital, Ruby was desperately needing us in Africa and now Jubilee had her own very serious situation going on and would need an immediate potentially dangerous surgery.

Literally within minutes of Dr. Pakhi's call, Kathi called to say that we had been granted an immediate invitation to get fingerprinted. With the girls and I already in Denver for Jubilee's testing, Dwight jumped in the car in less than an hour with the boys (Graham, Isaiah and Elijah) and drove the eight hours to Denver so that Emma, Dwight and I could be fingerprinted together. Autumn and Emma both needed to be fingerprinted since they were over 18 years of age and both were living at home.

Even though Dwight, Emma and I would all be fingerprinted that day, we would still have to wait for Autumn to get to Denver. We also had to find a skilled surgeon to do Jubilee's surgery as soon as possible.

Again, God would have to be working behind the scenes to figure it all out. Thankfully, after years of watching Him faithfully love our family, we knew we could bring our burdens to Him.

My head was swirling with so many serious concerns and no doubt, Dwight and I were both feeling the weight of all the serious medical situations we had going on around us. Our hearts were heavy.

After Dwight reached Denver with the boys, we drove to the Immigration office for Emma, Dwight and I to be fingerprinted. After we finished we headed back to the hotel to decide what to do next.

Our pediatrician had thought the surgeon in Denver would be calling imminently but that was not the case. Clearly, the Lord had another plan as the growth needed to be removed quickly.

The situation was shocking and the air was heavy as we stood in the parking lot deciding if we should travel home or wait in Denver for the surgeon's plans. We decided to head home. We would make other decisions once we reached there.

With two cars now in Denver, we were trying to decide who

should ride with whom, when Elizabeth cheerily shouted, "I know! Why don't the Chinese kids ride with dad and the Africans ride with mom?" Leave it to our sweet pile of kids to lighten the mood and fill the air with joy.

Uproarious laughter broke out as we piled into our two cars and drove eight hours back home to decide the next step toward surgery for Jubilee.

Once home we busied ourselves figuring out what to do about Jubilee's surgery.

Then, just three days after we returned home from Denver, Autumn, who by God's amazing grace had been working for years for the airlines and had enjoyed the perk of free flights, flew up to see Karl in the Rehab hospital. The following Monday morning, Vicki (Karl's mom) graciously drove Autumn from the hospital to the Immigration Office to be fingerprinted.

Autumn and Vicki had a difficult time finding the US Immigration Office but finally they were able to reach the building and within minutes Autumn texted me, "I'm out. My fingerprinting is done. We're going back to the hospital now."

Now remember, it normally takes 75 days to get Immigration clearance, right??

Exactly **EIGHT MINUTES** after Autumn texted me that she had just finished being fingerprinted and was leaving the immigration office, Dwight's cell phone rang. It was not a number he recognized. Answering his phone he heard a woman question, "Is this Dwight Saunders?" "Yes it is," he responded.

"Dwight, this is Officer McC from the Department of Immigration for the United States of America. I have been waiting for your daughter Autumn to come in and be fingerprinted. I see Autumn was just fingerprinted and I want you to know that I have granted Immigration approval to you and your wife - please go get Ruby Grace. I only have one request. Please email me a picture of Ruby at home, with weight on as she becomes the happy little girl with a family!"

Dwight started to cry as he promised Officer M we would do that! Then he called me, "We have Immigration approval!"

I started to cry, "Really? Really? You're not kidding me?" He assured me - it was not a joke!! God had moved in such a powerful way, I weep as I type. God had indeed been about our business as we had been about His.

Not 75 days.

Not 40 days.

Not 20 days.

Not one week.

Not three days.

Not even six hours!

Eight minutes!!!

Just a mere eight little minutes between Autumn's text and the Immigration Officer's phone call to Dwight.

Eight tiny minutes - shorter than some drive-through lines. God is the God of the impossible!! When He does something He does it with undeniable flair! And when He moves there is no arguing that it was ONLY God. Throughout scripture we are reminded how much God loves the orphan. God's word declares that He is a Father to the Fatherless and His love for the orphan is limitless.

God's deep desire is that each orphan know the love of a family. Why should we be surprised that He would provide an eight-minute time frame instead of 75 days for a dying, emaciated baby orphan girl? He just needed a family willing to bring her home. We had said, "yes" and He was moving heaven and earth to get her safely home.

Once again, we were reminded why we refer to Him as **"Our Miracle-working, Mountain-moving, Awe-inspiring, Gasp-giving God."** Eight minutes was a true "gasper" and He is the only one who can receive all honor, praise and glory! We stand in awe of His greatness and how He brought Officer McC to the right place at the right time for Ruby.

While God had been orchestrating that, He was also providing a skilled surgeon for Jubilee's much needed surgery. Through the blog world a woman, Christie, wrote to me and mentioned that her child had had the same tumor and that she knew of a surgeon in Stanford, California who was world renowned for his expertise. I called his office and in minutes was on the phone with one of the sweetest medical staff personnel I have ever had to deal with. I explained the situation and she immediately sprung into action.

She hung up to discuss Jubilee's situation with the surgeon. A few minutes later she called back. It was a Friday and she began with, "Well the doctor would like you here today, but since you are in Colorado, can you be here Tuesday morning? He will see Jubilee, assess the situation and we will have surgery scheduled for Wednesday."

I assured her we would be on the road by Sunday and would be in the area Monday.

I hung up and called Dwight and explained what she had worked out for us. The risk of Jubilee's tumor already penetrating the brain was extremely high. The surgery would be Wednesday, we would have a post op a few days later and as long as all was well, we could leave the area for home on the following Monday. That meant that Emma and I could leave for Africa to get Ruby once we were back in Colorado.

****

We are a large family and we love to do life together as a family as much as possible. The trip to Stanford would be a family trip. Our oldest daughter, Abigail and her family live in the San Francisco area and so this would also give us a chance to spend a bit of time with them. We needed to get packing!!

We were on the road bright and early Sunday morning. I kept in close touch with Autumn on how Karl was progressing in rehab in Denver as we drove the miles across Colorado, Arizona and into California. We talked, ate, laughed, sang, and played games as we drove the miles. There is nothing like a sweet pile of treasures on a road trip across the country. My heart was soaking up every minute. Although life had dealt some painful times, God's faithfulness has always been evident. We knew He would provide everything Jubilee would need in the days ahead.

Jubilee's surgery proved to be yet another miracle in the midst of all the others. Although the surgeon had to remove all of her inner ear, he found that the tumor had not yet penetrated the lining of her brain. It was miraculous, because the tests had seemed to indicate a very strong possibility that it had.

Faithful God. Moving on our behalf.

We all enjoyed spending a bit of time with Abigail, Ryan and Finn and as soon as we had the post-op visit done, we were on our way back to Colorado with only days till Emma and I would leave for Africa to get our tiniest treasure! We couldn't get home fast enough!

Chapter 3

Whispers

While driving home from California I busied myself making lists of what needed to be done before Emma and I left for Africa. We had less than a week to get ready.

A top priority was to prepare Ruby's room. Because of Ruby's health, we thought co-sleeping would be a necessity however, in my heart, I still really wanted her to have her own little special place. Silly as it sounds I was adamant that Ruby's room be decorated and a crib set up before I left. I reasoned that it was kind of my way of showing her how excited we were that she was home.

The kids and I went to a neighboring city and visited Hobby Lobby. Since we were living in a mountain town with a lot of Wild West flair we thought it would be especially fun to have a little cowgirl theme. Her crib and decorations would be set up in a little corner of our library, which was right across the hall from the master bedroom. It would be cozy and sweet.

Dwight and Graham had made the knotty birch bookshelves and cabinets that lined the wall of the library. Having a love for books, it was definitely one of my favorite rooms in our home. At least we would smile and pretend she slept there!

The girls and I found a few little red cowgirl themed items and the letters R - U - B – Y. After painting the letters red, they would be hung above her crib. But life sped by much faster than planned and I never got her corner decorated nor did Dwight get her crib up before we left for Africa. I was disappointed. I think down deep I felt that if I had the room decorated and the crib up, she would really come home. I guess I will have to confess that there was such fear in my soul that she would not live to get home.

I had slept little in the days since learning of Ruby. Even before the Director asked us to adopt her, I was so burdened with her struggles. I wanted her to live. I wanted her to tell the world about how God had rescued her. I wanted her to know the love of family and the joy of knowing the love of Jesus.

One of my most favorite verses in the Bible is Psalm 25:14, "He whispers secrets to those who respect Him." It is impossible to fully comprehend that the God of the Universe, the God who set the stars in place, the God who created mankind, the God who placed the majestic mountains above the land, the God who sent His son to die for us in our sinful state would want a personal relationship with us.

As a little girl, my life was wracked with abuse, heartache and trauma. I grew up feeling shame, fear, inadequacy and completely unworthy of anything, yet, He rescued me. He alone knows the depths of despair I had lived in for many, many years. He knows the inner being of me, and not only did He love me in the midst of it all, He rescued me, set me free and healed me. He did it all, because He loves me. And every single day He whispers to me.

As I ponder the thought that the God of the Universe promises that He whispers secrets to those who respect Him, I am awestruck. Usually in life, when someone tells another person a secret, it is most often something that is not for public information. That's why it's called a secret. Some secrets will eventually be told, but there are many secrets in life that will never be told.

To fully comprehend God's promise of 'whispering secrets to those who respect Him' seems hardly possible. Yet it is a promise of Hope, with only one contingency. The contingency is a personal relationship with Him in which we respect Him, obey Him and have a healthy awe of who He is and what He is capable of doing.

When I was just four years old I heard that God sent His only Son, Jesus, to die for me. I cried as I understood what He had done for me. I did understand sin. I had already been being abused for three years, so I was well acquainted with sin, shame and pain. I understood heartache probably more than many would understand in their lifetime. And yet, in the midst of it, God almighty provided a way of escape - not in the physical realm, but in the spiritual realm.

Even though I was just a little girl, I desperately needed Him. I longed to know not only that God loved me, but also I passionately wanted to obey Him and to grasp just how much He loved me.

I will never, ever forget that day, some 50 years ago that I understood that God sent His son to die for me. I wept as I heard. I invited Him to come in and save me, to forgive me for any sins I had committed and to take my life and use it. Even though I was just a little girl, I understood much more in life than I could even verbalize. And God in His amazing love, at that moment, gave me an ability to grasp something that completely changed my life: He would never, ever leave me. He would be with me, no matter what.

From that moment on, I prayed to God all the time. I prayed that He would use me. I prayed that He would be my best friend. I asked Him to help me to obey Him in a way that would always make Him proud of me.

Yes, it is probably difficult for many readers to understand how a four year old could really comprehend and have her life changed, but I am living proof that it is possible. From that day forward, all I ever wanted to do was to please Him. No matter what would come my way, my heart just always wanted Him to be proud of me.

The abuse I lived in didn't stop, but I now had someone to whisper to at night. God was up. He was listening. He was comforting me. He was whispering to me and even in the midst of all the shame, grief, heartache and pain, His love was powerfully evident to a brown-eyed, deeply hurting, painfully shy, little girl.

Fifty plus years later I can confidently say that had it not been for that very personal, very real encounter I had at just four years of age, I would not be who I am today. It changed the trajectory of my life in such a way that I shudder to think what would have likely happened to me had it not been for that monumental moment.

When I was in my early 20's I went for counseling to deal with the effects of the abuse and trauma. Two different counselors, independent of each other, told me that they could not believe that I was not institutionalized due to what should have been the lasting effects of it all. Yet because of the power of God manifest in my life from just four years old, I walk in His peace, His truth and His amazing love.

I know what I endured. I know what it was like. The only one who knows and was there was Almighty God. He has been my only completely faithful and trustworthy friend. My confidant and yes, He really does whisper things to me daily. I cannot thank Him enough for healing me emotionally, setting me free and tenderly loving me.

So it was that just days before Emma and I would leave to head to Africa that I was standing in my kitchen looking out the window doing dishes. We had lost our home and our personal belongings to a fire two years earlier and when we had rebuilt our home, although we changed the layout, we had made sure that the kitchen window faced the Rocky Mountains. Each day I would soak in the spectacular Rocky Mountain view and praise Him for His artistic hand in the picturesque scenery.

This particular day, just like every other, I stood looking out the window, stopping to enjoy the breathtaking view and lifting up praises to Him, "Thank you so much for allowing me to live here in the mountains. I am a mountain girl through and through. I love the beauty of your handiwork." When I paused in praising Him, I heard Him whisper very clearly, "Enjoy the view, because you will not be seeing it anymore."

All I could think was, "Wow. Really? I wonder what that means." I didn't feel fear or concern. I just knew that I had heard His voice and wondered what that meant exactly.

Close friends of ours, Gordon and Deb, had graciously and generously offered us their frequent flyer miles when we were getting ready to make reservations to go get Ruby. While getting ready to make the reservations, I had heard the Lord whisper that we should fly out of Phoenix, because Ruby would need immediate medical care. If I had put two and two together, I probably would have realized what His whispers all meant, but I trusted Him completely and I knew that when the time came, I would understand what that whisper about not seeing the Rocky Mountain view ever again had meant.

On another interesting note, as I prayed for Ruby, I never could picture her in our home. It actually frustrated me. Why was it that I could not picture her being carried in my sling around the house, sitting on our massive porch watching the kids romp on our three acres, nor could I picture her at church with us? I kept pushing the nagging thoughts to the back of my mind, for if I let them linger, it would have been very disconcerting to my soul.

Of course I didn't realize that in two and a half short months I would completely understand what His whispers were all about.

Instead I focused my attention on heading to Africa to meet the precious treasure who had stolen both Dwight and Emma's hearts and who we had been fasting, praying and earnestly pleading for since June. Emma and I could hardly wait!

Chapter 4

Does It Look Bigger?

Flying across the oceans and finally landing in Africa, Emma and I were on a determined mission, with one goal in both of our minds: Get Ruby safely to the United States as quickly as possible!

But for all the desire and need to get Ruby home, there was a very long list of steps that had to be completed before leaving the country could even be considered. Foreign adoption is not an easy process, even when a child is medically fragile. We already knew and understood this and we continued to pray for Ruby's protection given the state of her frail little body and the Hydrocephalus.

It was comforting to know that many people around the world were praying as we went. The vast majority praying specifically that the process would go as quickly and as smoothly as possible.

As I prepared to go to meet her, I had played through my mind, over and over, what it would be like to finally lift her tiny little body into my arms. I could not wait to hold this little bitty treasure that had occupied our hearts and thoughts for months now.

The long drive from the airport to the guesthouse where we would be staying seemed to take forever. We had decided we would drop our luggage off and then have the driver drop us at the orphanage. Nervously rubbing my hands together, I stared out the window. How would Ruby be when we arrived? Would she be desperately sick? Would she smile? Would she be aware that her mommy had arrived? Would she cry when I held her?

As funny as it might seem to those who have never adopted before, there is always one common question lurking in the back of a parent's mind as that mom, dad or both make their way toward meeting their child for the very first time. It does not matter how many times you have adopted before, it does not matter the age of the child, it does not matter how long you have been in process to bring them home and it does not matter how much paperwork and hoops you have jumped through to get to that long-awaited moment. Every parent wonders it: What if he or she doesn't even like me?

Just like everyone else, I wondered it, too, and told Emma what I was thinking. She shook her head, rolled her eyes and giggled. She was convinced that Ruby would love her mommy.

48

Reaching the guest house that would be our home for the weeks we were there, Emma and I dashed to our room, dumping our bags as quickly as possible, and ran back to the car to continue on to the orphanage. We didn't even bother to change our long overdue travel clothes. We just needed to get to Ruby.

Months of praying.

Months of sleepless nights.

Months of agonizing before the Lord.

Many days of fasting.

Mounds of paperwork on the United States side.

Finally, it was almost time to meet the little bundle whose life the Lord had lovingly spared - this precious baby girl whose story had been tugging at people's hearts around the world. The little treasure with the huge brown eyes, whose entire six-pound being had stolen our hearts. It was the final countdown to Ruby-time.

Within minutes of dropping off our bags I was following Emma through the security gate and into the orphanage compound. Emma, familiar with exactly where Ruby had been lying only a couple of months before, now led the way with me following closely on her heels. Where would we find Ruby?

Passing little children playing, small tots swinging on swings, each step my eyes scanning volunteers and orphanage mamas who sat near the babies lying on blankets outside. Suddenly Emma stopped abruptly in front of a large mat where at least eight tiny babies were lying and stooping down, exclaimed, "Here she is!"

I scanned the babies trying to recognize which little treasure was my Ruby. They were all so tiny and yet, as Emma lifted her up to my arms...I was taken back. I was not prepared for just how tiny her little body would be and how large her head was compared to it. Tears welled up in my eyes as I soaked in the beauty of this moment. Longingly loved, desperately wanted and passionately prayed for, it was finally her turn.

Ruby now had her mommy.

Emma snapped pictures of this monumental and life-changing event: Ruby was no longer a nameless, faceless little one in an enormous crowd of orphans. Ruby had been chosen. Ruby now had a family. Ruby would no longer wonder who cared. She would know. Her mommy, daddy, many brothers and sisters, they all cared.

She was wanted.
She was needed.
Ruby mattered.
Ruby was valued.

Staring into her sweet face I realized something powerful. Although Ruby had weighed six pounds at just thirteen months old when Emma and Dwight had found her, that was not really an accurate depiction. It was now clear to me that most of that six pounds had been the weight of her sweet head.

Brain infections and the Hydrocephalus had been ravaging her fragile being and had overcome her preemie size body. I was stunned at how disproportionate her head was to her body. My heart was so completely broken for all that she had endured over the last fifteen months. Abandoned. Alone. Waiting for someone to come rescue her.

As I cradled her in my arms whispering to her, Ruby began to whimper. It was the sound of someone in pain. Although I was trying to hold her carefully and gently, fully supporting her neck and head, no doubt, her head and neck had to be hurting. It was so unbearably large and how painful for her neck to bear the weight, even though fully supported!

I whispered to Emma, "Does her head look bigger?" She nodded affirmatively. We knew that the director had said that Ruby's head had grown larger and I had wondered aloud if Emma could tell a noticeable difference. Yes, she could tell, it was even larger than it had been 12 weeks before.

I found myself overcome with feelings of complete frustration for not getting to Ruby sooner. Although I knew in the depths of my soul that there was nothing I could do about it between finishing up our home study, fingerprinting, Immigration paperwork, Karl's accident, Jubilee's surgery and all the rest. My heart was wrenching as I peered down at my precious and very visibly fragile baby girl.

Ruby had needed us and yet she had been lying waiting, growing worse by the moment and we had finally just arrived. It was so incredibly upsetting to me. I just wanted to sob and sob.

But I had to pull myself together and be strong! This was definitely not a time for sobbing; there was work to be done. After spending some time getting to know my littlest treasure,

I carried her to the orphanage office in hopes of finding the Director to tell her Emma and I had arrived and would be meeting with our attorney that same night.

The Director was in and graciously welcomed us into her office where we sat and talked for a while. I thanked her profusely for allowing us the privilege of bringing Ruby home forever. I assured the Director that we would have Ruby to the States as fast as the African side could process the necessary paperwork.

Emma loved on the sweet babies while I changed Ruby and fed her. From here on out, we would spend every day getting all the necessary paperwork on the African side done while we lovingly cared for Ruby at every possible moment.

I laid hands on Ruby and prayed over her as I gently put her down late that afternoon. I prayed that God's ministering angels would protect her as I went to the law offices to see our attorney. I prayed that her crib would be filled with angels who would tend to her every need and that she would feel God's liquid love presence surrounding her. It was incredibly difficult to leave her behind. I could hardly stand it.

The orphanage mamas do the best they can, but there are many little ones whose needs fill their days. A medically fragile little treasure, who vomited with each feeding and required much individualized time, was not an easy task for someone dedicated to her care on a full-time basis. And to an already overworked orphanage mama, Ruby's specialized care was almost impossible.

Besides, everyone knows, no one is going to love a baby like his or her own mommy. Ruby's mommy was now here, yet completing all the paperwork would mean that I would have to leave her often as I was not be allowed to take her with me, which was agonizing to my soul.

Emma and I eventually left the orphanage to drive to our attorney's offices. I had never met our attorney before, but felt immediately comfortable with her. I showed her Ruby's picture and explained how time was of the essence. She took one look at Ruby's photos and clearly understood that Ruby's medical state was fragile, at best. She got out her legal pad and started writing down all the things that would be necessary to go to court. The list was long and pretty overwhelming to me. But no doubt, our attorney was a blessing and we are so thankful for her diligence in helping us through the process and ensuring that each step was completed as quickly as possible.

I had thought, given Ruby's fragile medical state, most of the necessary paperwork on the African side would have already been done by the orphanage. I was very wrong on that thought!

As it turns out, it was difficult to learn that nothing had been done to even begin the necessary paperwork. Nothing at all. If I had even thought once about it in the weeks before coming for

Ruby I would have written and asked the Director if this could be completed. Instead we would be starting at square one.

As in most international adoptions, a "Finding Notice" must go into the local newspapers, which meant we had to take Ruby to have her picture taken so it could be published with a notice from the orphanage, in the unlikely event birth family would want to come forward and claim her. After the Finding Notice is published, there is a wait time allowing any relative to come forward. This was one of the things that I should have asked to be done prior to my arrival.

Then there was another factor that also needed to be wagered in. In many developing nations, just finding a copier or printer can be a problem and at times even electricity to run a copier or printer can be a problem.

The day that we went to get Ruby's picture taken the orphanage mama assigned to Ruby's care, Mama Naomi, accompanied us. Ruby was primped and looking so beautiful. She loved being in my arms and I firmly believe that God had given Ruby a clear understanding that I was her mommy and we had come to rescue her. I also believe that Ruby completely remembered Emma.

Emma, Mama Naomi, Ruby and I walked to a village not far from the orphanage. We found a little photo studio at the back of a hairdresser's salon that was willing to take Ruby's picture and print it while we waited. I ordered several pictures, as it seemed likely that we would need some for her passport. As it turned out, we still needed a different one.

After getting her picture taken, we walked slowly back to the orphanage. I hated not having her with me all the time. No matter how caring an orphanage is, it is no replacement for the love of a mommy.

Once back, I went to show the Director Ruby's picture and to see if the Finding Notice had been written. The Director was not in and we were told it would have to wait until tomorrow.

Placing Ruby in her crib that night was so troubling to me. Many of the children at the orphanage were sick. Ruby's weakened body was so susceptible to every single germ. Any infection she got could go straight to her brain. Not only had the Hydrocephalus compromised Ruby's brain but also so had all the subsequent brain infections. It was extremely concerning to my soul to know that little treasures were so sick all around her.

The next morning Emma and I were up bright and early as we headed to see Ruby and check on the progress of the Finding Notice.

I held our tiny Ruby and watched the Director work away on her computer trying to get the Notice all typed out. Once finished, she explained that the Finding Notice would need copies, although there was no copier at the orphanage. We would have to find a copier.

I wanted to go get the copies made immediately, however, the village was out of electricity, as were the surrounding villages. Talk about frustrating! The power was not expected to be on for at least another day.

I questioned if we might be able to take the Finding Notice somewhere further away that had electricity in an effort to get copies made. She nodded. Yes, I could try to do that, although Ruby was not allowed to come with me. Of course we knew we needed the papers copied before the ads could be placed. Time was of the essence.

I struggled leaving Ruby behind. It would have been so much better for her safety and our bonding to be able to run around getting the papers together. But Ruby was not allowed to go.

Emma and I found part of the neighboring city still had electricity some distance away. We were able to secure the copies and as quickly as possible head back to the orphanage.

As we arrived back at the orphanage we learned that there was not one person at the orphanage who would be able to take the Finding Notice along with Ruby's picture to each of the local newspapers. I asked if it would be possible to call someone we knew to come and help me by taking them to the proper places. I was pretty certain that this friend of ours would be able to help us and I was fairly sure that he could use the money I would pay him. The Director agreed.

I phoned our friend and before long he had met us, secured the papers, been given money by me and had hopped on the back of a motorcycle to get the papers where they needed to be. The Notices had to run for two weeks. Once the Finding Notice had run for 2 weeks, we would check that part of the process off our list.

I wanted to cry. If the Finding Notices had been done before we came, while Ruby was desperately sick and waiting for us we would be two weeks further down the road. How I wished I had inquired while still in the States. But here we were starting at the very beginning of the process. It was so upsetting! Everyone who knew Ruby knew that she needed to get home as soon as possible.

After our friend took the Finding Notices with Ruby's picture attached to each, we learned that the report from the local officer had not yet been done either.

I also had no idea how to find the local officer, or who the local officer even was for that matter, but I knew I needed to find out as soon as possible, because all of this would take valuable time, which Ruby definitely didn't have any extra of.

As it was, we learned that a local government officer had been assigned Ruby's case. This same officer needed to come to the orphanage to meet her and evaluate the legitimacy of her abandonment. The social worker at the orphanage gave me his name.

Since the Lord had warned me that this process would be a battle, the failure of most of the paperwork being done was not surprising in light of His whispers. I was fasting often since arriving in Africa and knew it was time to fast even more. We needed the Lord to clear the path in a mighty big way.

Regularly Emma and I would go back to our attorney's office to see about the progress on the court papers that needed to be filed. Our attorney asked for copies of the pictures I had shown her of Ruby so she could attach each to the court file, clearly visible to each person who would handle Ruby's case. Our attorney felt that the pictures would be beneficial in helping those who would handle Ruby's file to understand that this was not just any adoption, but this little girl needed immediate medical attention.

In order to get the pictures for our attorney, Emma and I would need a jump drive to transfer the pictures from my computer, enabling us to then take the jump drive to a shop that would print out multiple pictures.

Emma and I hired a driver and set off for the city to find a jump drive. As it was, the power had again gone out in much of the villages and even into the city, which only complicated matters. If the power was out for days, it would set back every bit of the paper process considerably.

Each day counted and actually each moment mattered. We had to work as fast as we could. This was not a time to kick back and let each piece work itself out. We had to figure a different way.

After some hunting we found a jump drive. What much of the western world doesn't understand is that there is no major office supply chain store next to your national pet supply store in a plaza next to the nearest mall. Not even close. Each piece of paper, each pen, each notebook, each jump drive is a rare commodity in a developing nation and each piece of office equipment is an ultimate rare privilege.

We are so grateful for the shop owners in developing nations who have dedicated themselves to earning their livelihood from start-up office supply shops. These shops are such a blessing to all the necessary parts of the adoption paper trail.

The roads back to the orphanage were jammed with cars and the time it took to get back was unbearably slow. I had to push out of my mind how long I had been gone from Ruby. If I were to dwell on it, it would have been overwhelming. Knowing each moment I was gone from her she was not getting the mommy lovin' she desperately needed was so painful to my heart.

As each detail seemed to be such a struggle and the process seemingly moving at a snail's pace, Emma and I committed to fasting regularly, believing that God would use this much-needed spiritual discipline to supernaturally push the process forward.

Chapter 5

One Amazing Smile

The guesthouse where Emma and I were staying often served as an impromptu hub for ministry minded individuals from many countries to connect and get to know each other. One morning before heading to see Ruby, we were eating breakfast and met a small mission team from the United States. One of the couples had been to Africa before, the other had not. We were chatting as we got to know each other when the conversation rolled around to them asking us what we were doing in Africa.

Emma and I shared Ruby's story and mentioned that her orphanage was close by. We were surprised to learn that although one of the couples had been to Africa before, they had not ever been to an orphanage to serve. They were equally surprised to learn that an orphanage was in close proximity. We asked them to stop and just listen. "Do you hear the children's voices?" They could hear them once we pointed them out. They were shocked to learn that we stood that close to the place where little treasures were in desperate need of love.

They asked if Emma and I would be willing to take them to the orphanage to show them the children. We agreed and set up a date and time. They were eager to see exactly what an orphanage could possibly be like.

Of the two wives, one had longed to adopt for years. The other mentioned that her husband would adopt in a heartbeat, but she liked the way her life was. She felt that she would have to pray long and hard to see if it was something that God would ever want them to do.

****

I have met hundreds of women who are crying out to the Lord to change their husband's heart toward adoption and here was a husband who desperately wanted his wife's heart to be willing.

I realize that as an adoptive mom ten times over, I just can't shy away from the plight of the orphan. I promised myself many, many years ago that I would be their voice.

As with many of the conversations I have had over the years, I am always perplexed by the notion that adoption is something we need to ask God if He is in favor of.

From a Biblical standpoint, there is absolutely no need for discussion as to the propriety of adoption. God's word references adoption over and over. From basically the beginning of scripture the plight of the orphan is mentioned and spoken of in the context of our need to care for them. The parable of the Good Samaritan found in Luke 10: 25 - 37 gives strong confirmation what the intention of God's plan for each of us is. Simply put, when we come across a need, no matter what we are doing, we are to stop and meet that need.

The religious leaders spoken of in Biblical times were just too busy to meet the needs of the man beat up and dying on the road. We read the passage and shake our heads thinking, "How could they just walk by the man left bleeding and dying on the road?" Yet everyday there are treasures in orphanages around the globe, treasures in our foster care system and treasures even living on the streets - all of whom are God's deepest concern and many folks turn the other way and just walk on by.

What if the Good Samaritan had walked on by so that he could go spend some time praying about whether he should help or not? What if he had spent his valuable time arguing all the reasons why it would be okay to just continue on his way? After all, he was already heading to an appointment and he actually was probably pretty busy! What if he had reasoned that likely someone else better equipped would be coming by soon? What if that Good Samaritan had thought, "it's not really my problem anyway"?

Every day millions of Christ-followers around the world move about doing life and don't think much, if at all, about the orphan crisis. Countless millions of capable individuals, upon hearing of the orphan crisis, quip things like, "Wow. That's too bad." Others shake their heads at the prospect of opening their hearts to care for someone outside their family. Still others even criticize those who are adopting or fostering or going on mission trips. Could it be that resistance to orphan care is really the fear that in stopping to acknowledge the need, one might actually feel the tug to do something themselves?

Once a friend remarked to me as I mentioned the orphan crisis, "Well that's just your thing." No, actually, dear friend, it's God's thing and He doesn't give a lot of room for any of us to shrug a 'whatever' when it comes to caring for little ones in need.

There's been some who have said, "That's your gifting Linny." I always smile at that one. As if caring for a child in need takes some special skill. No actually, it just takes putting ourselves in another's shoes.

Caring for the orphans is not a gifting or a deep spiritual ability to do something extraordinary. It is merely seeing the vast needs around and deciding to meet a need at the expense of our own time, commitment and resources.

I am convinced that if we are breathing, we are compelled in some way to answer the call to care for the orphans. Do all have to adopt? No. Of course not! But we all have to do something.

Should many more adopt then do? Personally, I think so. There will always be opportunities for cop-outs in life and I fear that someday many will stand before Christ and will see the thousands of faces of orphans flash by on "the big screen" and remember that they turned away and pretended the orphan crisis didn't exist.

As for Dwight and I, the pleading eyes, the prospect of empty tummies writhing, along with the ever present and always desperate longing to be in a family just cannot be ignored. We have to do something!!

What are other possibilities, if adoption is not truly an option? Of course, we feel that one tangible way is regularly scheduled mission trips to love orphans is paramount! Loving, caring and praying over the little ones, just like our Ruby, is a necessity!

There are also countless ways to lend ongoing support to those who do open their hearts and homes to precious treasures. Including verbally cheering them on, making regular meals for families that open their homes, buying clothes, gathering a small group of people to clean a house for a large adoptive family, offering babysitting for parents to have a coffee date on a regular basis, or lending a hand in any way possible. The possibilities are truly limitless!! Actually, I'm pretty sure this is what God meant when He said, "Care for the orphans and widows!"

For illustration purposes here's a story that's fresh in our lives. By God's divine orchestration, when we first moved to Phoenix, I met a precious woman, Lynne, who winters with her kind-hearted husband, Bill, here in Phoenix each year. After meeting we kept in casual contact.

As the Lord would have it, our recent move to a completely handicap accessible home took us to the very neighborhood Lynne and Bill live in each winter. I was excited to tell her that we would be nearby when they arrived for the winter!! Not long after she arrived this year, she asked if she could provide art lessons (for free!) to our children each week for the winter. She is a retired public school art teacher. I loved the idea!! She has ministered to our family more than she could even begin to imagine by loving our children, lending a hand and doing what she does best - teaching art! Our kids look forward each week to their art day and have done incredibly amazing art projects with her! She has been Jesus' hands and feet to our family this winter!

There are so many possibilities to minister to the orphan or the families who open their homes to them. Dream!!

****

Getting back to the women who wanted to go to Ruby's orphanage with Emma and I....

The morning dawned bright as we met the ladies to walk to the orphanage nearby. I could not wait to introduce my Ruby to them!

Ruby had not been very responsive in the weeks that I had been in Africa, although I had spent hours and hours snuggling, holding, singing "Oh How I Love Jesus" and whispering tender words to her, she did not really respond. I knew that it might be a long journey and that was okay, but like any parent, there is a longing to have some kind of response from your child.

This particular morning, Ruby was on her side facing the wall in the corner of her crib as I reached to lift her tiny, frail body into my arms while telling her joyfully, "Ruby, I have brought friends to meet you!!"

Imagine my joy when as I was turning her body toward me, Ruby's face lit up with her first ever smile! It was huge!! It spanned her entire tiny little face. I giggled with joy. "Oh Ruby!! You know me. It's mommy. I love you forever!"

The ladies oohed and aahed over my sweet baby girl. They then went on to see how they could help with the other little ones. I knew God was going to work in their hearts as they served. I hope one day I will hear just what He did.

I had seen it so many times before because something very powerful happens in the supernatural when willing hearts dedicate time to serving the needs of the orphan. One just cannot walk away unchanged.

Chapter 6

Where is it?

Much of the developing world does not have access to the care that Western nations have if one has Hydrocephalus. Africa though has an exception to this medical emergency.

When Emma and Dwight had first thought (and it was subsequently confirmed) that Ruby had Hydrocephalus, Dwight had gone to the computer room and began to research Hydrocephalus treatment options.

As the Lord would graciously have it, a missionary doctor had begun a hospital in an East African country that was actually on the cutting edge of Hydrocephalus research and was foremost in medical expertise surrounding it. Imagine our joy to find that this very cutting-edge Hydrocephalus hospital was only about seven hours from Ruby's orphanage.

While Dwight was still in Africa, he went to the Director of the orphanage to tell her about the missionary hospital dedicated specifically to the treatment of Hydrocephalus. He gave her all the information he had found out about it.

At that time, Dwight asked the Director if we could pay for Ruby to go to this hospital to be evaluated and treated. As Dwight was leaving the country for his next Legacy Conference he actually left money with the Director to cover all the necessary expenses to pay for transportation and the Hydrocephalus surgery for Ruby. He promised to send more when he was home. Having told the director repeatedly not to allow money to stand in the way of Ruby's care, he had assured her that we would pay for anything Ruby needed.

Before he left Africa he went in three times to remind the Director that we were willing to do anything for this sweet baby girl. Anything! He said that if any need arose, just to let us know and we would wire more money for her care.

Weeks later, when we had committed to adopting our Ruby, the Director took Ruby to this same missionary hospital to be evaluated and to see what they could do for her. The Director told the missionary hospital's surgeon that Ruby had a family coming for her and upon hearing this; the missionary hospital immediately contacted us. They wrote to us daily and even sent a picture of Ruby lying in the hospital. She looked like a little fragile doll, tiny and so strikingly beautiful. We cried when we received the picture, so grateful for their communication with us and so thankful that she was being evaluated and expertly cared for.

After careful examination, an MRI and after a few more days at the missionary hospital, the hospital staff emailed both us and the orphanage Director saying that it was determined that Ruby was just far too frail and emaciated to consider doing brain surgery on her. They were insistent that Ruby would have to go to a highly specialized nutrition ward at a different hospital, in the same city as Ruby's orphanage, where she would get specialized care to ensure weight gain.

So when Emma and I arrived in Africa, there was no doubt that Ruby, having spent time in a nutrition ward had put on a bit of weight and did not look quite so emaciated. The Director of the orphanage told me that the missionary hospital would not consider surgery for her Hydrocephalus until she had gained a significant amount of weight.

As the days passed working on the necessary paperwork, Emma and I would check Ruby's fontanel daily and suddenly it seemed much more puffy. Although I am definitely not a medical professional, but merely a silver-haired mom of many, I have felt and seen plenty of fontanels. I knew that Ruby's fontanel was far too large in circumference and far too bulgy for a 15 month old.

I shared my concerns with Dwight each day. We knew that the missionary hospital had not wanted to see her until she had put on a significant amount of weight, however, the bulging fontanel warranted a neurosurgeon's expertise.

Dwight had all the information about the missionary hospital on his computer and so he emailed with one of the surgeons there, explaining that I was now in Africa with Ruby, she had put on some weight and that her fontanel was bulging. Thankfully Dr. John remembered Ruby and told Dwight that he would see Ruby the following Friday, which was only days away. Dwight and I were so grateful that Dr. John, a man who had dedicated his life to caring for those with Hydrocephalus, would actually be the one to personally see our little treasure.

So it was, that only two weeks after landing in Africa, Mama Naomi, Emma, Ruby and I, along with a driver loaded into a car to make our way to the missionary hospital to meet Dr. John and have him re-evaluate Ruby's situation.

As the driver wound his way through the spectacularly picturesque African countryside we were in awe. Having always dreamed of going to Africa, I could not believe I was finally experiencing this amazing privilege. It was truly my dream come true! Each mile we drove we passed more huts with thatched grass roofs than we could have ever counted. We found the beauty of the little villages completely indescribable. I was enamored with the natural simplicity of it all.

But while we drove the seriousness of the situation began to sink in. It may sound silly, but in the thrust to get adoption paperwork tended to, I had not really stopped to think about what was about to happen. Without warning, I realized that our fragile little baby girl was on this faraway continent and Emma and I would be alone with her facing the trauma of brain surgery, while being so medically fragile. Suddenly, it all seemed so completely overwhelming.

Although Dwight was at home in the States with the other kids, how I longed for them to be here with us. I missed them all so much. And I really, really didn't want to be in Africa alone with Ruby's upcoming brain surgery.

Reaching the missionary hospital, the driver pulled through the massive gate and rolled to a stop in the little parking lot. As we stepped out, I was immediately impressed with how very clean the entire campus was. The massive buildings, which had been meticulously built, formed almost a square. Inside the square was a beautiful center courtyard. Simple signs hung on each building, clearly marking what clinic specialty one would find inside. The entire property was filled with well-manicured tropical flowerbeds, each adorning the orange brick facilities. I was completely overcome with what a peaceful place this was and I felt an assurance that could only come from the Lord. This highly specialized missionary hospital had been anointed by God and no doubt, God's spirit of peace and healing rested on the entire hospital grounds.

As we stepped inside to register, person after person remembered Ruby, clearly indicating that her little six pound self had made quite an impression on each one's heart. One by one we found each hospital employee to be warm, gracious and helpful. Emma and I were overwhelmed by their love for our little bundle. Dr. John had ordered another scan as soon as Ruby arrived. I was so grateful that I was able to stay with Ruby as it was performed.

After Ruby's scan Emma, Mama Naomi, Ruby and I sat outside Dr. John's office waiting to meet with him. We weren't there long when Dr. John greeted us. He was gracious, kindhearted and gentle as he welcomed us into his office.

A familiar white glass hung pressed against the wall on one end of the little room. Dr. John began immediately explaining how Ruby's situation was unique and how emaciated she had been when he first saw her. He further detailed that because of her frailty surgery had not been possible, as she would likely not have lived if it had been attempted.

He explained a bit about Hydrocephalus.

Here's a little medical explanation of Hydrocephalus direct from the Hydrocephalus Association's website:

*Hydrocephalus comes from the Greek words **hydro** meaning water and **cephalus** meaning head.*

Hydrocephalus is an abnormal accumulation of cerebrospinal fluid (CSF) within cavities in the brain called ventricles. Cerebrospinal fluid is produced in the ventricles and in the choroid plexus. It circulates through the ventricular system in the brain and is absorbed into the bloodstream. This fluid is in constant circulation and has many functions, including to surround the brain and spinal cord and act as a protective cushion against injury. It contains nutrients and proteins necessary for the nourishment and normal function of the brain, and carries waste products away from surrounding tissues. Hydrocephalus occurs when there is an imbalance between the amount of CSF that is produced and the rate at which it is absorbed. As the CSF builds up, it causes the ventricles to enlarge and the pressure inside the head to increase.

Dr. John said that Ruby was still so small to really consider surgery, yet because we had come many hours he felt he should go in and perform a fenestration surgery. He went on to elaborate that the type of Hydrocephalus that Ruby has is called, "Multiloculated Hydrocephalus".

Multiloculated Hydrocephalus: A complex condition that occurs when bleeding or infection causes scars within the ventricles of the brain. The scarring creates many small pockets of CSF that do not connect with each other. In the past, doctors treated multiloculated hydrocephalus by placing a separate shunt in each pocket that held fluid. Now, using an endoscope, they can make small holes in the pockets. This connects the pockets enabling the areas to "communicate" with each other so a child would need only one shunt.

Dr. John also explained that it would be far too risky to put a shunt in right now. Although Ruby would definitely need a shunt in the United States, the risks were too great for her to go back to the orphanage and then to possibly wait weeks until we returned to the States. A shunt could malfunction or even get infected, either of which would be too great of a threat for tiny little Ruby.

Dr. John said that the only thing that might help alleviate some of the pressure would be to fenestrate some of the many places that were holding the water, allowing these places to flow back and forth, creating an ability to drain some of the fluid. He said several times, "You have come so far, I feel I cannot send you back without doing something for Ruby."

He went on to mention that because of Ruby's Hydrocephalus, we would need to live in close proximity to a neurosurgeon when we returned to the United States.

Dr. John's words took me by surprise. It never had occurred to us that we would need to live near a major Neurosurgical center. Although several of our other treasures also have special medical needs, we had always driven to wherever they needed care. Some we would take four hours away and others we would take to Denver, eight hours away.

The small city we were pastoring in did have a hospital, but it was not equipped with any type of pediatric specialty unit, and definitely not a pediatric neurosurgical unit. Dr. John made it clear again as we sat listening: Ruby's situation could change at a moment's notice. If Ruby's situation did change, we would have to be in close proximity to a major pediatric neurosurgical facility immediately or we could risk losing her.

Dr. John's words replayed in my head over and over. Of course I knew in my heart what that meant. Ruby was ours and if she needed to live near a neurosurgeon, we would do anything for her, even if it meant moving to the ends of the earth to keep her safe. I knew Dwight would be in complete agreement when I told him what Dr. John had said.

With that proclamation Dr. John turned to face the large white glass on the wall. He opened the envelope, which contained Ruby's films and quickly snapped the first film against the brightly lit glass. He began to explain that most people with Hydrocephalus have one place with water on the brain. Seldom there are two places with water and it was almost unheard of that there would be three places of water. He did not count the number of places filled with water; however, I could tell that there were many more than three.

I have had Multiple Sclerosis since I was in my twenties. I have seen many, many MRIs of my own brain. By no means an expert on MRI or CT films, I am at least familiar with what the brain looks like on the films. As Dr. John talked, he was putting up film after film and I kept thinking, "But when is he going to get to the films with Ruby's brain on them?"

Reaching the bottom of the pile, he started back again. One by one. Slowly. Each film I stared, wondering, "Where is it? Where is her brain?" I kept watching, staring, waiting. Each slide that Dr. John put up and each one that he put down, my eyes darted the entire slide, "When is Dr. John going to get to the slides of her brain?" Intently I watched. Patiently waiting. Wondering.

But no such slide ever came. Not even one. Dr. John went back and forth through each one. Over and over showing me all the places filled with water in her brain. My eyes stared at the slides.

As I look back, I can better understand how God created our own brain with the ability to enter a denial mode. I knew what the answer was going to be, and in that denial mode I just didn't want to ask Dr. John straight out why we couldn't see Ruby's brain.

It was then that suddenly I remembered the words of the African doctor who had looked at the CT scan that Dwight had taken her for, "She will never do anything. Don't even bother with surgery. There is nothing there. There's no point in wasting any time on her."

And at that exact moment, as this reality was colliding with my passionate, pleading mommy heart, a protective position, like none I have ever experienced before, rose from within. It was with a relentless determination that I would firmly declare in my heart, "Nothing is going to hurt this baby girl of ours. She is far more vulnerable then we had ever begun to imagine. She needed us even more than we could have dreamed. We would protect her with everything in us and we would do whatever needed to be done for her."

This understanding further drove the point home. Ruby was a rare gem from the very heart of God. If He had allowed her to survive her abandonment in an African garden, exposed to the blistering African sun, Almighty God surely had a very specific plan for her life, regardless of what any MRI or CT scan showed. Regardless of what any medical professional thought. Regardless of how the world viewed those medically fragile.

At that moment, hope from the Lord rose from deep within my soul and instantly the Lord brought to mind something that, literally days before leaving for Africa, I had seemingly, almost accidentally, stumbled upon.

The thing about God is that nothing is accidental with Him. He is always at work behind the scenes and so it was with a story that I had came upon just a few days before leaving for Africa to bring sweet Ruby home.

With all the circumstances that we found ourselves confronted with just before leaving for Africa, I had not been reading much of the news online. But for some rare reason, days before leaving I happened upon a story that stirred something deep within me. I actually whispered to the Lord, "There is something significant about finding this, isn't there?" Although He did not whisper back the significance, I paid close attention.

The story was of a man who had had significant brain trauma, which in turn had taken most of his brain. Although his CT scans and MRI films showed that the vast majority of his brain was missing, this man had married, he and his wife had had children and he held down a full-time job. It was one of those stories where people hearing it stand back and marvel. Against all the odds humanly speaking, he had overcome, by the power of God, and was living proof that God could do anything.

Sitting that day, studying Ruby's films, I suddenly remembered the story of the man whose MRI showed that he basically had no brain and simultaneously one of my favorite verses in the Bible (Isaiah 49:23) flashed into my mind, "Those who hope in Him will not be disappointed."

We would choose hope; hope in the God of the Universe, the God who had accomplished undeniable, life-changing miracles for centuries, hope that He could not only do anything but that no doubt, He could certainly work in our sweet Ruby's life. God could do it any way He wanted. He could make her brain become whole in a instant, He could cause a new brain to grow where there was none or He could leave her MRI scans 'empty' but yet have her life accomplish miracles.

We had only ever hoped in Him and we would continue to hope in Him.

Almighty God could do it any way He chose. But God would do it. I just knew it. Ruby would far exceed what the original doctor had said!!

Her life already had value, no matter what and I knew in my heart of hearts, at that very moment, that she would accomplish miraculous things. She had not died in the garden abandoned and alone. God had rescued her for a very unique and specific purpose. He had called her life out of the darkness because He had a plan.

We would have the privilege of having a front row seat in all that God was going to do in our Ruby's life, and I knew that I knew that with our hope firmly placed on Him, just like every time in the past, He in His faithfulness would never, ever disappoint us.

****

The morning of the surgery my heart was filled with deep concern. Never in my wildest dreams would I have imagined that at 53 years old, I would be in Africa, cradling my sweet fifteen-month-old baby girl as she waited for brain surgery at a remote missionary hospital.

When we surrender our lives to the Lord, the only thing that is predictable is that His plan is definitely very unpredictable! It was crazy all the places God's path would carry us. I still could not believe that I was in Africa, far from my husband, as our daughter was facing her first brain surgery.

I would have to repeatedly bring myself back to the fact that my trust rested in the Lord, who clearly had cared for Ruby to this point.

I loved that the missionary hospital saw hundreds of Hydrocephalus cases each year. As we waited in Ruby's little room, Emma and I took turns reading the Bible aloud to comfort and bring peace. Mama Naomi was the only one who had been allowed to stay with Ruby the night before. She was so gentle with her. It was comforting.

As we waited for her surgery time, there was a slight knock on the door and upon opening it we found the sweet face of a tenderhearted patient liaison. She had come to pray with us before Ruby had surgery. Wow! What a blessing. She and I talked at length about the power of God and really, by the time she left the room, I felt that I had made a new friend.

When it was near time for surgery we were asked to bring Ruby across the grounds to the Surgery building. I cradled her in my arms as we walked. Her beautiful little self had already been through so much. Emma and I fought the tears.

Entering the surgical building, we stood inside leaning against a wall waiting for Dr. John. I prayed softly over Ruby and sang "Oh how I love Jesus" time and time again.

After a few minutes, Dr. John appeared and walked over to where I held Ruby, and lifting her from my arms, he smiled and said, "We're ready!" Through tears in a barely audible voice I spoke, "Take good care of her. We love her so much! We have many praying around the world for your hands as you operate!" Glancing back he smiled and nodded.

We slowly made our way back outside where we sank into chairs overlooking the beautiful grounds.

I phoned Dwight to tell him that she was now in surgery.

Oh the powerful emotions that flooded our souls!! It was all so surreal.

Eventually Dr. John made his way out to where we sat. The surgery had gone well. He had fenestrated through some of the walls so the water could communicate with each other. Things had gone well. She would be moved to ICU and we could peek in on her later.

A few days later Ruby was stable enough to leave and start the journey back to the orphanage. There was still so much paperwork to do before she could head to the United States with us. The brain surgery had bought us some much needed time and now we had to move into high speed!

Chapter 7

There Truly Are No Words

As a mama to several special needs treasures, it is hard to grasp sometimes the treatment of people with physical or mental challenges. Over the years I have had, on occasion, to pull myself together as I have witnessed mistreatment of human beings. I have seen with my own eyes people abuse special needs treasures many times.

And yes, sometimes it has been a total stranger against someone in our family. There are no words. The old "kids will be kids" doesn't cut the mustard with this mama, because what I've found is that often those "kids" turn into 'adults' who, having gotten away with obnoxious and hateful behavior as children continue on as adults to perpetrate that same behavior toward other human beings.

If a parent isn't going to call a child on hateful behavior, then for goodness sake, rise up witnessing adults - someone has to!

On more than one occasion we have experienced hatred

toward our children. Sometimes we have witnessed hateful mocking from other children, but even, sadly, we have also had it come from adults.

Once, a few years back one of our children with designer genes was trying to communicate something with us. We were in a train station, with only a few people standing around. A grown man, observing our sweet daughter's labored language skills, turned to the people he was with and after imitating our daughter, laughed uproariously. My eyes welled with tears.

How could a grown man find our beautiful daughter's obvious efforts to talk to us so entertaining that he would use her as an example of humor? How was it that, at her expense, he would think it appropriate to make others laugh? How could he fail to understand that her precious smile was not an object of ridicule? To this day, I still shake my head. We could make excuses for him, but that would actually be shameful. He was a grown man! His behavior was atrocious.

There have been other occasions as well. But none stand out quite like what happened one dreary and rainy day while bringing Ruby home...

As the days had turned into weeks, it became clear that we would not be heading home anytime soon. In Africa, each piece of paper is an effort to obtain and the process is arduous. Not impossible, but definitely rarely smooth.

One particular Sunday afternoon Emma and I were at the orphanage playing with the babies and loving on our Ruby. Volunteers seldom come to help on Sundays so we were spending the day enjoying the toddlers and babies, ministering the love of God to each of these little ones.

It was rainy and rather chilly and I had Ruby wrapped in several receiving blankets as I held her close and whispered to her about the goodness of our God. Her head was covered and her frail being barely visible amidst the gobs of cotton flannel fabric.

Ruby always felt so cold in those early days and I commented to Emma that I thought maybe, with her significant brain trauma, there was a very real possibility that her internal thermometer didn't work quite right either.

Emma was on the floor with a dozen or more little ones climbing all over her, calling her "Mama Emma." I was sitting, snuggling Ruby close and talking to the little ones playing around me as a woman, about my age, came walking into the room.

I'd never seen the woman before, but she was dressed up in her Sunday finest. She looked lovely. Truly, she was a woman of class and refinement. Dressed perfectly, her shoes even complimented her suit.

I smiled at her as she approached and the woman smiled back brightly. We made a tad of small talk as she came closer toward where I was sitting. She spoke articulately and mentioned that this was her first time visiting the orphanage. She had heard a lot about it and came to see it for herself that day.

As she looked about the room asking questions, she also began inquiring about some of the little ones playing nearby.

We talked for a bit and after a few moments had passed, always anxious to show off my beautiful littlest treasure, I pulled the blanket back and boosting Ruby up a bit while beaming ear to ear I exclaimed joyfully, "This one is mine! I'm in the process of adopting her and taking her back to the United States. Isn't she gorgeous?"

Instantly the woman's mouth dropped as she saw Ruby's head swollen with the Multiloculated Hydrocephalus. Her expression, which had been pleasant, turned to instant disgust, almost hate-filled.

Just like that.

My mind raced!

Truly, I was bewildered. What was her new expression for? Had this same woman not just been smiling with me and enjoying a friendly, albeit brief, conversation?

At that moment, the meticulously dressed woman now stepped closer and lifting her hand, literally flicked Ruby's head as she said something in a foreign dialect! Her hand actually snapped the side of my precious baby's head with the swiftest of movements. I was so taken off-guard I didn't know what to do! She turned abruptly on her high heels and left the building in a whirl.

Tears welling in my eyes, I could not believe I had just witnessed, in my own arms, such treatment of my precious, barely surviving baby girl. The woman, for all her fanciful clothes, did not understand the beauty of my daughter. Nor did she understand that although my daughter's head was larger than others, Ruby is the most beautiful baby girl we'd ever seen.

Ruby is been made in the image of our powerful and mighty God. Ruby's face looks like His. God does not measure our value by the size of our head or the color of our skin or the shape of our eyes.

No doubt, the woman's outward action was a symptom of a much larger heart issue. Her devaluing of humanity in the frailest of forms grieved my heart. To this day I still cannot believe anyone would commit such a heinous act against a teeny-tiny baby in the arms of her doting mother.

I had suspected some disdain for Ruby when out with her to process paperwork, but was clearly beginning to understand that Ruby would never have the adoration of many in her home country due to her Multiloculated Hydrocephalus.

Let me be perfectly clear, ignorance is not only found in Africa, but it is found all over the world and yes, even in the United States. It comes in all forms.

After that horrific and abusive incident, when introducing Ruby and telling people her name I attempt to include this in the introduction: "We have named her Ruby because we believe she is a precious gem from the heart of God. Did you know that a ruby is actually more valuable then a diamond?"

I purposed in my heart, from that day forward, to educate all who came in contact with our little tiny treasure of her infinite value to all mankind. Ruby's life exudes the grace, blessing and favor of God. Oh that every person of every nation would understand the value of all the precious, special needs gems around the world!

Chapter 8

Struggles

One day, in the midst of the unending adoption paper trail, Emma began to feel very sick. As each hour passed, she grew increasingly worse. Ruby was at the orphanage and Emma was now terribly ill. I literally ran to spend time with Ruby and ran back to check on Emma as quickly as I could.

We had now been in Africa long enough to guess, with the symptoms she was experiencing, that the likelihood was strong that Emma had something that needed some medical attention.

All night long I woke to check on her and each time her fever was raging. In the middle of the night she even seemed to be kind of delusional. Oh gracious, I needed her to be well!

It happened that I had an appointment at the US Embassy in the morning and had to be up to leave very early. I knew there was no way Emma could make the trip so I asked our African friend to come and sit with her as I ran to the Embassy. I was concerned to leave her alone as sick as she was.

When I returned to our room a few hours later, I found it difficult to wake her. I talked to our friend and together we decided it best to take her to the clinic. We thought there was even a possibility that she had malaria.

After some tests, it turned out Emma had a very bad case of food poisoning! The good news was that after just two doses of antibiotics she began to feel remarkably better...and within a couple of days she was back to her spunky self! What an answer to prayer!

As the days continued to pass, Emma and I persisted at working diligently on all the necessary paperwork.

One of the things we learned we needed was for the US Embassy's representative to come to the orphanage and do a careful and complete examination of Ruby's abandonment.

Those who were assigned the normally routine tasks of getting each document prepared {like the Embassy representative} weren't given the information necessary to understand just how fragile Ruby's health was. To most she was just another name on a piece of paper.

As time was crucial for Ruby, all delays were potentially extremely costly to her health. We were so grateful for the many friends and family who were praying. We are convinced that it was the direct prayers of orphan loving blog friends and family that brought sweet miracles along the paper trail.

One day we were at the orphanage and a woman who worked in the office came running to me and said, "The man from the Embassy is here! Hurry!! Quick!! Come meet him! Bring the baby!"

I went to meet the gentleman and quickly introduced him to my sweet Ruby. He gently shook my hand and upon seeing her enlarged head he lowered his voice and softly spoke, "My friend had a child born like that. I know how important it is to get medical care. As soon as I get your paperwork, I will process it quickly."

I hadn't asked the man for any favor in any way. I didn't have to beg! God had orchestrated the events, including this man knowing a friend who also had had a child born with Hydrocephalus, which in turn stirred his heart upon seeing my precious baby girl. None of that would have happened if the orphanage worker hadn't connected all the dots and ran to get me.

Clearly, the power of praying people and a loving God who answers prayer!! Our ever faithful, miracle-working God was surely at work.

Another evidence of God's movement happened a few days later. I had been given the name of a man that I needed to meet with to have papers drawn up to go with the filing of our court documents before we could proceed to get a court date. I had never heard of the man, had no idea of how to reach him nor did

I know where to find him.

We felt like we were on a human scavenger hunt! If we had set about to look for him, I would have had to leave Ruby at the orphanage to search. However, God was moving behind the scenes on Ruby's behalf!

That particular day, while preparing to go back to our room for the night, we happened toward the gate and found a man putting his motorcycle helmet on as he also was preparing to leave the orphanage. I had not seen him before and had no idea who he was. He was a handsome young man who was dressed as a professional. He even had a tie on!

Suddenly I felt like I should introduce myself to him. Under normal circumstances I tend to be rather shy, but this was such a strong urge, it could only be the Lord. I thrust out my hand as I spoke, "Hi. I'm Linny." He shook my extended hand and told me his name. Gasping, I nearly shrieked, "You are the man I am supposed to be meeting with to get a document drawn up for our court appearance and I had no idea how to find you!" He grinned from ear to ear at the craziness of it all.

Elaborating, I went on to explain to this government officer Ruby's situation. I asked when he could come and meet her and do the necessary paperwork. He was very polite and said that I would need to come to his office to be interviewed. Hmm. That was not normal protocol from what I had heard, but whatever he wanted, I was willing to do. I asked if I could come that very day.

He graciously informed me he was leaving to go out of town and would not be back for a full week.

Those who know me, know that I am usually not one to beg or be pushy in any way. But knowing he was leaving to head out of town for a full week was just one more date that would be pushed further away. Although totally uncharacteristic of me, I resorted to begging him to allow me to please come that day. I begged with all my might! It was not pretty!! All he did was smile and say, "No". I even begged more. I explained how Ruby's situation was desperate! Again, he politely told me no. Oh well. It couldn't hurt to ask, or in this case, beg.

We set it up for the following week. I was grateful that the Lord had allowed me to meet him in an impromptu way so that the visit could be set up. This meant, that once our lawyer had the paper, and all the other papers, her office could finally submit them and then obtain a court date.

This still was taking way, way, way too long!

We needed to pray earnestly and fast some more and press on!

*****

In the meantime our attorney told me that she had spoken to the judge and he wanted a letter from a neurosurgeon at the government hospital stating that Ruby needed care in the United States.

I questioned if it was possible that a letter from the missionary doctor would be okay. Having met the doctors at the missionary hospital and knowing that they were sympathetic to Ruby's plight I felt they would be willing to write such a letter for the Judge.

However, the Judge insisted that a letter from the missionary hospital neurosurgeon was not the letter he wanted. He wanted it to come from the Government Hospital.

I had no idea where to start with that but we fasted some more and set off with Ruby in our arms and with Mama Naomi trailing along to figure it out. Emma and I prayed for much favor as we went.

At the Government Hospital we had several surprises. Some were sweet surprises others were not so sweet.

First off, although we had arrived early, we found row upon row upon row of neatly placed simple wooden benches. The benches were almost completely filled with approximately 300 people. No doubt, each clearly in line to obtain medical care.

I almost fell over when I saw the line. Of course, the entire gathering stared at us. We were obviously not what most saw on an average day as they waited at the hospital, not to mention that I'm sure many were wondering why we had Ruby with us.

Someone near a desk motioned for us to go sit down. We turned toward the line of benches and at exactly that moment, out of nowhere an African man grabbed my arm. I turned and he motioned, without any words, to follow him.

So we took off following this man who had come out of seemingly nowhere. I was wondering where he was exactly taking us but since he had offered no explanation, I didn't ask any questions. It was actually kind of comical! No words, just a motion of "follow me" to which we turned and began to follow a complete stranger!

He stopped abruptly at the door to a tiny, tiny examining room. He opened the door and spoke in the local dialect. The person in the room glanced up and motioned for us to enter.

The man stepped aside so we could go inside as he waited outside. The man inside happened to be a doctor. When he gave me his attention I told him I had been sent by a Judge to secure a letter stating that the baby girl I was adopting would need care in the United States.

He told me that he could not write the letter because he was merely a General Practitioner and not a Neurosurgeon. I explained that the Judge did not require it to be written by a Neurosurgeon just a doctor at the Government Hospital.

This General Practitioner then said, "Well I have a friend who is a Neurosurgeon, I will send you to meet with him." He scribbled some words on a small piece of paper and handed it to me. He then told me where I would find his friend.

The friend was on the opposite side of this enormous Government Hospital campus. So off we went, hiking the campus looking for the Neurosurgeon. When we arrived at the place where we were to find him, he wasn't there.

Some medical staff present told us that they would call and find him. I was so grateful for their helpfulness. Upon hearing where we would now find him, we set off to catch up with the Neurosurgeon who was supposedly waiting for us.

Except that when we got to where he was supposed to be, which of course was on the opposite side of this sprawling campus, he was now nowhere to be found. We were told to stand waiting in a ward filled with very sick people lying on black plastic covered mattresses.

We didn't mind waiting; my only concern was all the sickness surrounding us with a fragile and very susceptible Ruby in my arms.

Literally, hours passed.

The Neurosurgeon finally appeared and informed me that he was just an intern and he would not be able to type such a letter. He then continued on that the Chief Neurosurgeon would see us when he was done with surgery. I wasn't sure what to do. We had already waited approximately six hours with many extremely sick people all around us. I hated to keep waiting. But I hated even more not having the paper that our attorney had told me the Judge wanted.

So we waited.

Finally, we were called to a little office down the hall. There were two nurses already in the office. One smiled at me. The other just stared. And in walked a very tall man whose stature spoke of power. His entire being seemed to shout, "I am the boss!"

His glasses were down on his nose and he bent his head down so he could easily peer over his glasses to see me. Staring at me, he barked, "What do you want?"

Knowing that this ominous man did not appear to be a chatty fellow, I quickly explained that Ruby was very sick with Hydrocephalus and that my husband and I were in the process of adopting her. Getting right to the point, I stated that the Judge had wanted a letter from a doctor stating that she needed care in the United States.

I was completely unprepared for what happened next.

This man's face began to turn red with anger. His facial features contorted as he raged and screamed, "She doesn't need to leave here! She can be cared for right here! She doesn't need to go anywhere. Our country can take care of her!!"

He was screaming so loudly that people were now looking toward this little office that was completely surrounded by windows. I stood still with tears welling in my eyes.

I wasn't about to argue with him about how although it might be true that this hospital could take care of her, there was not a soul who had stepped forward to care for our sweet baby girl on a day-to-day basis. I also didn't think it would be the right time to mention the lady who had flicked her head in disgust at the orphanage the previous Sunday.

As I stood listening to his explosive tirade, my eyes kept welling with a steady stream of tears until they plunked from my eyes and ran down my cheeks as he spewed venomous words.

I prayed as he carried on.

Finally, he stopped. One of the nurses next to him looked at me as if to say, "I'm so sorry." The other looked like she had enjoyed his bout of rage.

I wasn't sure what to say, but having spent my early years being bullied and abused by men I just couldn't walk away. I'm not sure what response he wanted, but I just asked very quietly, "Do you really find that much pleasure in screaming at women?"

He didn't say a word, but the look on his face was pure hatred.

I turned and moved quickly to the elevator doors. We couldn't get out of there fast enough. There would be no letter from a Neurosurgeon for the Judge and we would have to just pray that the Judge would be okay with that.

****

The very day the government official had said that he was going to be back in his office, I phoned him.

However, I think he had been kidding about what day I could call, because it took four extra days for him to return. And that was beyond frustrating.

When I finally reached him he told me that we would need to set up an appointment to come in to be interviewed. In keeping with the whole "Africa is never in a hurry" fashion, he told me that we would have to wait for the appointment for several more days.

When the day finally arrived, Emma, Ruby, Mama Naomi and I went together for the interview.

It turned out, that there was only one real question that was pressing on this gentleman's mind and basically the entire reason for the interview: Why did we really want to adopt Ruby?

I was actually quite taken back. It was very difficult for me to understand how someone could possibly *not* want her, let alone wonder why we would want her! We saw Ruby as a vulnerable, teeny-tiny, precious treasure! How could anyone not want to have the privilege of loving, protecting, nurturing and caring for her?

I did my best to try to explain it to him. He sincerely couldn't understand at all why we would want to adopt her and I believe he truly wanted to understand from my perspective.

As I gathered my thoughts and shared my heart I choked back strong emotions several times throughout the time spent with him. I shared how our other children, several of whom were also considered special needs brought us such joy. Not only did we have the privilege of protecting and providing for them but we felt we were honoring God's request: "Do to others as you would want them to do to you."

He intently listened to each word I spoke. He didn't ask many other questions. He just had to hear for himself. The time with this young man gave me insight into the plight of the special needs treasures in developing nations and Third World countries. The vast majority of adults just can't even begin to grasp how someone would actually seek to bring home anyone who needed anything, let alone someone who would need round-the-clock care.

I could only pray that my words had conveyed God's heart to this young man. When we were done talking he closed his files and said, "I will submit your paperwork. Thank you for helping me try to understand. And thank you for doing what you do."

I assured him that my husband and I were just really two very selfish people who wanted to hog all the joy. He smiled and kind of laughed. Obviously, he thought I was kidding.

I wasn't.

****

When every last piece of paperwork was finally in the hands of our attorney, she submitted Ruby's file to the courts.

I was so excited!

However, it was then that she called me to tell me the news. The Court Recorder, who takes the file, officially stamps it and sets a court date, had had a death in the family. She had gone to the village for the burial and wouldn't be back anytime soon.

I questioned our attorney, "What does 'anytime soon' mean?" Our attorney said she had no idea. Sometimes the burial could last for weeks.

Weeks? Seriously?

We didn't have weeks!! Ruby needed to get on a plane and get to the Phoenix neurosurgeon yesterday!

Days passed and the Court Recorder still had not returned. I finally went to our attorney's office and asked, "Isn't there someone who fills in for her? Like what if she was suddenly in a terrible accident, then what would happen? Surely someone would fill in for her."

She smiled and answered, "No, there is no one to fill in for her. Even if she were to be sick and in the hospital, we would all just wait until she came back to work."

We asked others to pray and fast with us. The only thing that would breakthrough this crazy seemingly unending string of obstacles would be the power of our loving God.

****

As the weeks passed, it became increasingly difficult for us to leave Ruby each night when we would have to head to our room in the small guesthouse nearby. Even though darkness was falling as we were leaving each night and I knew it was not at all safe, I really just couldn't stand leaving her behind and would drag my heels till I finally laid her down.

Just as equally heart wrenching was the thought that if Ruby understood anything of what was going on, she was wondering why I left her each night as well.

We had been told by the desk clerk at guesthouse where we stayed that it was not really safe for us to walk back and forth at night, but neither Emma nor I knew any other way we could do it.

One night after cradling, singing and praying over our sweet Ruby I gently laid her down and turned to see it completely dark outside. A shiver ran down my spine. I was surprised. It was really, really dark.

Apparently time had gotten away and we were much later than we had been before. I went to find Emma who was helping with several other little ones. I told her we had to leave quickly.

As we hurried out into the smoke filled streets it was actually kind of difficult to see. A flashlight would have helped on the uneven ground.

Emma was in front of me on the crowded sidewalk, but I was following close behind. I didn't want her to get out of my sight but I was also trying to watch my footing.

Without any warning I felt a firm, strong hand grab my arm! A man's gruff voice shouted, "Come with me!" Turning, in a flash, my eyes met his and I jerked my arm with all my might, shouting, "NOOOO!" My heart was pounding as I took off running. I no longer cared about my footing or the uneven road or even the people I was bumping into...I just desperately wanted to catch up to Emma.

Emma had not known that the man had grabbed me, but as I came up behind her I whispered, "A man just grabbed me, walk faster!"

Emma started to almost sprint. We were both very shaken by the time we reached our room. Although we knew that we had been uncomfortably close to danger that night, we also knew that the Lord had protected us from any harm. We would choose to praise Him and thank Him instead of focusing on what could have been.

Chapter 9

She's Ours

Just as leaving Ruby each night was increasingly difficult, leaving her during the day to process paperwork was not any easier. I hated it all!

Our most favorite days were the days when the paperwork necessitated Ruby accompanying us and yes, we tried to think of any reason that Ruby needed to come with us!

We were able to take Ruby to several places: the attorney's office a few times, to have passport pictures taken, to the doctor's office for a required exam, to the Embassy appointment and for both court appearances. Of course, Mama Naomi came with us as well for almost all of these until I had obtained official custody of our little treasure.

Ruby loved being in my arms and my arms loved having her in them. Her teeny-tiny self fit beautifully! Emma joked that she had to beg me for her turn to snuggle with Ruby. I readily admit that I was rather selfish with her!! I couldn't help myself!! I was smitten.

Finally it was Ruby's turn to go to court!! Finally! We were anxious. Ruby was all dressed up in the prettiest teeny size 0-3 month dress. She looked so vulnerable and yet so very beautiful.

Our appointment was for 2:00pm. As we were ushered into a room to wait, we caught a glimpse of the judge just receiving a lunch tray. He would be taking lunch and then he would proceed with all the cases on his docket.

Ruby still threw up every time she ate and although I tried my best to be prepared for that, as we sat waiting she vomited all over her pretty little self and all over me. It seeped through my clothes. I had to laugh as I tried to clean myself up!! If only my empty-nesting peers could see me now!

When it was time to move into the courtroom, we found that there were many cases ahead of ours. Ruby would be last. We waited our turn for hours. I was so thankful I had packed many bottles.

The judge finally called us up to his bench. He asked a few questions and then gave me an assignment. He wanted us to tour historical landmarks in an attempt to learn to love our daughter's country. He told us to bring back certificates stating that we had toured the landmarks. He would render his decision in two weeks.

Although we had prayed for favor with the judge, it didn't seem to matter that Ruby's health was compromised. I was so disappointed! I thought we might have her case expedited when he saw her fragile state.

Turning to leave I glanced at my cell phone and found that it was now after 9:00 pm. Ruby's orphanage social worker had been at court with us, but when the proceedings went past the dinner hour she had left to tend to things at her home. She mentioned as she was leaving that she would leave the man to wait for us who had driven her to the court, so he could drive us back to the orphanage. I wasn't sure what I thought of that since I did not know him at all nor had I ever seen him before.

But 9:00pm was not the time I could easily be looking for a ride so this driver would have to suffice. The court building was completely dark as we made our way out of the courtroom. We are so spoiled by the well-lit office buildings (even well after business hours) in America.

We had to tediously fumble our way down the stairwell in complete darkness except for the light of our little flip cell phone. It made me nervous carrying fragile Ruby without being able to see clearly. Not to mention that going down stairs is the most difficult thing for my legs due to the MS. In keeping with their normal behavior, they trembled as I made my way down the two flights of dark stairs holding tightly onto our little princess.

Entering the parking lot and trying to see in the darkness, we noticed a man had jumped out of the driver's seat of a car across the parking lot and waved to us calling, "Madam, I am to drive you!" Since there was no other car in the parking lot with anyone in it, we guessed he was the right guy. We told him the name of Ruby's orphanage and we were on our way.

The streets of this African nation seem never to sleep when circumstances necessitated being out at night. Tediously the car made its way through the crowded streets toward Ruby's orphanage. Out the window of the car we saw literally hundreds of people walking along the side of the road in the dark.

I'm already not a go-out-at-night kind of gal in the States, so this all left me kind of unsettled. I would much rather prefer that all of us be tucked in for the night long before this very dark hour. Especially given what we had already experienced.

As the driver drove, we tried to look for some familiarity in the roads as he made his way through the city streets. Glancing over at Emma I mouthed, "Do you recognize this way?" She slowly shook her head from side to side and mouthed back, "No."

The driver had now turned on a road that seemed to almost be leading into the countryside. It didn't feel right and then suddenly, without warning, the driver slammed his car into park in the middle of his driving lane as throngs of people streamed by.

Literally one minute we were driving down the almost country road going to who knows where and the next he had slammed the car into park. There was no one immediately in front of us so we were bewildered. I looked at Emma, my eyes questioning, "What in the world is he doing?" Wide-eyed she shrugged at me.

Next he opened his driver door and mumbling something in his native tongue he hopped out of the car! Emma and I turned to each other staring and my heart was definitely starting to pound loudly. We had no idea where we were and it was now 9:30 at night in a country that was not our home on a road we definitely did not recognize.

He went to the trunk of the car and flung it open! What was he doing? My mind was racing. Locals were coming by and looking in our windows. To say that we felt vulnerable would be an understatement, especially given the time!

It was then that we realized that he had run out of gas and was grabbing his gas can. The problem was that we were in an almost country area. There was no gas station for some distance! We would have to sit and wait and pray!

I phoned Dwight and told him that we were sitting on a road with no street lights, it was kind of rural around it, locals were streaming by, peering into our car windows and we had no idea where he had gone, other than for gas.

If we had thought about walking {which we weren't that crazy!} we would not have even known which direction to go!

Dwight prayed with us and called a few close friends to pray as well. Many people in foreign countries think that Americans are wealthy and they can easily become victims of robbery.

Although I could feel my heart racing I told Emma we needed to sing some worship songs. So ever so quietly we sang worship songs and waited. Probably 45 minutes passed and finally the driver reappeared and put the gas in the tank. We were on our way and eventually reached our room. It was an adventure, but one that we would have been okay to do without. We also vowed to never use that driver again. Ever.

The weeks slowly moved as we waited for our day to finally go back to court. Although it seemed like the Judge would have to take pity on Ruby and move in our favor, I had to fight anxiousness and we definitely fasted and prayed.

Thankfully the Judge's decision was in favor of Ruby's best interest and we left praising the Lord. Finally!! Finally!! Finally!! We were overjoyed. I phoned Dwight to tell him the wonderful news. We officially had a new one-year old daughter!

****

On a side note, we have continued to keep in touch with the attorney who handled Ruby's case. She told me that when she sees the Judge he always asks how Ruby is. She commented, "The Judge has told me that he has two favorites from all his cases, and one of them is Ruby. He looks forward to hearing how she is doing regularly." It truly seems that Ruby is always a favorite of anyone who has the privilege of spending time with her. Such a victorious story!!

Every bit of Ruby's life is a testimony to the love and power of our great God!

****

It would take a few days for the court to actually have the documents signed by the judge, but we were now on the 'home stretch'.

I asked the Director if I could please take Ruby now with me to care for 24/7 and she declined approval. The Director wanted the actual court documents. We would still have to wait! Pleading did nothing. And yes, I wanted to scream!! I hated it with every fiber of my being.

A couple of days passed and finally we had the official court documents that proved I had custody.

I was giddy and phoned the Director! I asked if we could please process whatever needed to be processed so that Ruby could come with me. She told me that since it was Friday night, she was off the following day and that if it was going to happen on the weekend, it would have to wait until Sunday morning.

I'd love to say that I was just fine with that, but that wouldn't be true. I wanted my precious little girl being cared for by the only person who had committed to love her - me!

As I gently placed her in her crib at the orphanage that night, salty tears fell from my eyes. "Sweet girl, you are mine! Even the courts say you are mine, but I can't take you just yet."

Ruby's health was already very, very compromised and the last thing she needed was to spend her days and nights in a place with 50 other kids exposed to who knows what!

Imagine how distraught I was when the very next morning I arrived at the orphanage and found most of the little treasures extremely sick.

I would call my feelings at that point: righteous anger! Ruby's system was already very weakened and the last thing she needed was exposure to a multitude of varying germs or worse yet, any bacteria!

I held her all that Saturday praying and pleading with the Lord to protect her. As I prayed and sang to her that last night before lying her down, I whispered, "One more night sweet girl. One more night!"

Sunday couldn't come fast enough and papers in hand, we were at the orphanage not long after the first morning light.

The Director needed to be called and came a couple of hours later after learning that I was waiting. She took the documents I had brought. I then signed some papers as well and went back to dress Ruby in a pretty dress since she could finally leave with us that day.

Although we weren't ready to get on the plane yet, we were nearing the end of the very long paper process. Emma and I were gleeful, giddy, and downright ecstatic!

I was so relieved to have her out of the sickness and in my arms forever. Emma and I had noticed, after returning from Ruby's brain surgery, that Ruby's fontanel actually was better. So now that she was officially ours, we were filled with such relief that she could leave! No doubt the fenestration surgery had bought her some valuable time! We also noticed that Ruby hadn't been thrusting her head back and forth side-to-side quite so much - which to me meant that her head had also felt better.

However, the very day we left the orphanage with her in my custody, I was not prepared for how suddenly and drastically her health changed!

That joyous day Emma and I had decided to hire a driver and head to a little sandwich shop to celebrate Ruby being ours for good! There was such sweet joy in knowing that Ruby was finally in my arms to stay. She was really ours - forever!

Suddenly, as we sat eating, Ruby began to thrust her head side to side, with such force, my eyes grew wide! She also began to feel feverish and my heart began to race! For weeks we had spent our days hurrying to get Ruby to our arms and here she was finally in our arms and almost instantly showing signs of being very sick.

I was distraught!

As we sat at the cozy African sandwich shop I could feel Ruby's temperature literally spiking in her frail little body. She no longer wanted to even sip her bottle. She thrust her head side to side. She then vomited all over me - which in her case was likely a sign that something was amiss in her brain, especially as she thrust her head side to side with such force!

Emma and I talked and decided we should pay quickly and head to the British clinic to see what they thought. If the missionary hospital that specialized in Hydrocephalus had not been so far away we would have taken her straight there.

This entire situation confirmed in my heart that they weren't kidding when they said we needed to live in close proximity to a major neurosurgical facility. And at this point I was thinking that after returning to Phoenix, we could buy an RV and live in the hospital parking lot!

Ruby's situation was not like any one else we had ever known. Her health could deteriorate before our eyes - in minutes! The risk to her life was so real, I felt like I really could vomit myself.

We hurried and paying our bill headed straight to the British medical clinic.

Once at the clinic the doctor examined her, ordered some tests, took her temp (which was very high) and after some consultation decided that likely she had yet another infection in her brain - which she was still very susceptible to and likely caused by the sick ones at her orphanage.

The reality of Ruby's situation was that with each brain infection there could subsequently be more brain loss. We had to get the infection under control as soon as possible!

I could feel myself starting to crumble in panic. I had to remind myself - the Lord still had this, no matter what the circumstances looked like. I had come to know Him as Jehovah Rapha (the God who heals) and there was no doubt that He was more than capable of healing our tender, fragile baby girl.

I phoned Dwight to tell him what was going on and to ask him to pray and get others praying. We needed that fever to come down and the infection to go away as fast as it had come! I also knew I had to remain strong and there was no way I could cave to doubt. Although her high fever, coupled with her head thrusting was not helping my heart to feel peace.

I began to softly pray a verse that has long been a favorite of mine: "You, Lord, will keep me in perfect peace, because my heart and mind is stayed on you." Isaiah 26:3

I whispered it over and over. Eventually peace came. I had to trust.

The doctor talked at length with me. He felt that it was likely from her symptoms and the test results that she did, indeed, have another brain infection. He thought it best to put an IV port in her tiny arm and put some fluids in to hydrate her as well as give her some antibiotics through the IV port. We would bring her back every day to have more medicine put into her little IV port.

Emma and I held her still as the nursing staff worked extremely hard to find one of Ruby's microscopic veins in her tiny, gaunt arms. To watch it all was agonizing. I softly sang, "Oh how I love Jesus".... and our precious baby girl cried and cried and cried big ol' tears as the first nurse tediously worked to get that needle into a vein.

Unfortunately after more attempts than I could possibly count - for all of the poking and prodding in Ruby's hand, she still was unable to reach a vein. I finally asked if someone else could possibly try. I appreciated this nurse's steadfastness, but at this point, maybe someone else had more experience with easily putting an IV needle into probably one of the tiniest veins anyone had ever seen in this small hospital setting. The second nurse did indeed have better success and we all breathed a sigh of relief. The Lord had been gracious!

Finally, with the needle in place they made a little board to firmly secure her wrist. It was horrible to watch it all.

Often as a parent we want to take such painful times from our children. I had never felt such angst at what Ruby's delicate little body was enduring. She was so weak and so very vulnerable, I was willing to do anything to keep her from suffering anymore but the only thing I could possibly do was to pray and fast for her healing. Emma and I decided we'd better do both.

Chapter 10

Fleeing Under
The Cover of Darkness

Without a doubt, the rescue of Ruby was personally one of the most truly intense seasons of my life. It was complicated by unforeseen and unanticipated circumstances which if God had not rescued in each situation; the outcome could have been tragically different.

There is no doubt that Emma and I were praying and fasting regularly for God's wisdom, His protection and His divine direction over each detail, whether known to us or not.

After the long evening at the British clinic the three of us settled in for sleep. Ruby under my mosquito net with me, her little hand strapped to the makeshift board that was supporting her IV port.

I tried to sleep, but found myself so restless. I'm sure Ruby's health was foremost in my mind, however, it felt like something else was going on.

I know 'the feeling' well. Usually when this happens I am unable to put my finger on it precisely and so all I can do is pray.

That night I tossed and turned. Praying intently in the spirit and questioning in my heart, "What is my sleeplessness from Lord? What is going on?" I knew something was wrong; I just had no idea what it was. Ruby was snuggled against me and I was so thankful for that. I didn't need to wonder how she was, she was right beside me and I was completely relieved! Finally!

But something else didn't feel right. I knew in my spirit. I kept praying. I was thankful that I was fasting. It helps me to hear His whispers more clearly, although I didn't hear any whispers that night. And although He was silent, it was not for my lack of asking.

I was very grateful when the morning light began to dawn through the curtains.

As soon as we had dressed we hired a driver to take us to the British hospital for another dose of IV meds for Ruby. We kept thanking the Lord for the port, which enabled her meds to be dispersed easily.

The night before, while at the hospital having Ruby assessed, I had seen a young woman who was an inpatient in one of the little hospital rooms. My heart had been broke when I saw her. She was young, perhaps in her 20's. She was beyond emaciated. Her hollow eyes had stared at us while Ruby was being examined. This young woman's skin tone was a sickly green color. My best guess was that she was dying of AIDS.

Realizing we would be going back to the clinic daily for Ruby's IV meds to be administered, I was grateful. I wanted to meet this young woman and perhaps even visit with her. I hoped to be an encouragement to her. She looked so dreadfully lonely. Her very being spoke of complete hopelessness.

So on our way to the clinic we stopped at a little grocery store to gather a bouquet of flowers for this frail, gaunt, and what appeared to be, dying woman. I desperately longed for her to know the enormous love of God - just the way she was! No matter what the circumstances were that had brought her to this point, He deeply loved and cared about her and He definitely wanted her to know it!

That day I was able to give her the flowers we had brought and spend some time talking with her as Emma held Ruby waiting for the IV meds to drip through her port. Talking with this young woman proved to be a wonderful blessing and, yes, she was dying of AIDS. I was able to tell her of our faithful God's deep and abiding love for her. She told me that she wanted to spend eternity with this loving God that I was telling her about. She prayed with me and invited Jesus into her heart.

****

On a side note: On a subsequent mission trip, this young woman phoned my African cell phone. Although I was not in the country, Dwight was and remembered her story. He invited her to come to dinner with the team he was leading. She came and shared how my visit had brought her hope! Oh how God desires that we each know His unfailing love and once we experience it, we spend our days telling others of it.

****

After Ruby received her IV meds that day, we headed back to our room at the small guesthouse that had been our home for the last five and a half weeks.

We were settling in for the afternoon and suddenly, without any warning, something drastic happened.

Circumstances and details cannot be shared. Forgive me. However I cannot tell the story of rescuing Ruby without alluding to this horrific situation, because the reader must understand that this was the most intense battle of our lives!

As this unimaginable situation was unfolding I was able, by God's miraculous grace, to think with enough clarity to dial in desperation our longtime missionary friend, Abby. The situation was unfolding and I was able to press speed dial. She shouted into the phone that she would be there as fast as she could.

Before Abby's arrival I had to make some fast decisions. I prayed and pleaded with the Lord for wisdom: "God help! What should I do?"

As I moved in the direction of what I thought was best, suddenly I stopped completely and in an almost shout, I literally about-faced and did something completely different! I knew at that instant that this new plan was the Lord's perfect direction.

I had such holy God-inspired, completely unwavering boldness as I took authority over what was transpiring.

Truthfully, as a human being I do not think of myself necessarily as brave, however, what came out of my mouth was the most courageous, most fearless and most audacious words I have ever spoken in my entire life. The words came out in such a tone, as the unimaginable situation loomed, that there was no denying, "This will end and it will end now!"

Since it was so uncharacteristic of me, I knew the words and the tone in which I spoke them were firmly and loudly being declared from the very heart of Almighty God!

In the meantime our precious missionary friend had jumped on the back of a motorcycle and came immediately. She was at our side within a matter of minutes. That alone was miraculous! Abby courageously responded to our need and clearly was sent from the Lord to minister in a powerful way!

All I wanted to do was call Dwight, but when I looked at the time and saw it was the middle of the night in Colorado I knew that if I phoned and woke him, he could have had heart failure with the news of what had just occurred. I could not risk him learning of this most dramatic event when he was not fully awake!

No doubt, God had indeed protected - He had rescued, but no man would want to know what had just happened to his wife and daughters!

Abby stayed with us until her husband, David, could arrive as well. We were huddled together in our room praying and praising Almighty God that He had given me the complete about-face direction or the results would have been disastrous!

After a few hours together our missionary friend spoke, "You are no longer safe here. You must move and find somewhere else to stay." They offered their home, but we felt we needed somewhere further away.

So as the afternoon light faded into darkness, we threw all of our belongings into our suitcases. With the help of her husband, we loaded our things into a car being driven by someone they knew well and trusted. They then led us under the cover of darkness far away to a place of safety.

When Dwight woke for the day I was able to tell him what had happened. Although Dwight was in utter shock and disbelief, he was so grateful for the way the Lord had instantly changed the direction I thought we were supposed to go to deal with this most terrifying circumstance! There is no doubt that our powerful God had circumvented my immediate response and His authority had completely overtaken this dreadful situation.

Since we had fled under the cover of darkness, Dwight phoned the guesthouse staff and explained why we had to leave quickly. They were distraught at what had happened! He was then able to pay our bill on line.

I humbly stand in awe of what our powerful God did that day. The results would have been utterly disastrous had we proceeded in the direction of what I had originally thought best, but Almighty God had thwarted it all by His divine intervention.

Recalling the events that day, I am reminded of this verse:

"Man plans his ways, but God directs His steps." Proverbs 16:9

Looking back, there is no doubt in my mind that when I couldn't sleep the night before, the Lord had been preparing me through prayer. Because this situation, which could have turned catastrophic in a moment, was averted by His holy intrusion into the unforeseen circumstances that unforgettable day.

Mark my words, Emma and I both agreed: We would never, ever be the same again.

Chapter 11

Scars

As I mentioned before, while preparing to leave for Africa, the Lord had whispered to me that the spiritual warfare to bring Ruby home would be like nothing I had ever encountered.

Of course, I had no idea what exactly that would entail, but I was so thankful that I recognized His whispers. Although I didn't relish the idea of intense struggles to rescue Ruby, I was thankful that He had warned me. It enabled me to prepare myself through prayer and fasting. Besides, I was convinced that He also wanted me to have a heads up so that I would not shrink back in fear!

Clearly the warning meant - He would prevail, but the battle would be fierce!

When encountering spiritual warfare, we must have our hearts clear and in tune with Him and His will. I decided when He had whispered the warning to me prior to leaving for Africa, that I would fast regularly before going and while there. I would pray and fast for meals and some full days. I feel so much more confident spiritually when I am fasting. I am thankful for this regular spiritual discipline in my life that I have been doing since I was a young girl.

Knowing that the Lord had spoken clearly that the spiritual warfare would be unlike anything I had ever seen before, I kept wondering, "But why?" This would be our 8th adoption!!

No doubt, the Lord had orchestrated a ministry through the blog world for us to advocate on behalf of the orphan and vulnerable street children around the world, yet, it seemed with this clear heads up that there had to be another key element that I was missing.

Why Lord? What was so unique this time around?

Why was the rescue of Ruby full of so many obstacles? I knew there was something that I couldn't yet put my finger on. Every now and then I would ask Him, while fasting, as the days passed and turned into weeks in Africa. He was silent each time I would ask. I trusted that one day He would reveal the 'why'.

But once settled into our new hotel and reflecting back on the horrific circumstances of the day before, which caused us to flee under the cover of darkness, I shuddered in bewilderment. I knew things were going to be intense bringing Ruby home, but never could I have even begun to envision the terrifying events of the day before. God's grace truly had sustained us, but still I was at a loss. What in the world was going on? Why was the battle so intense to get Ruby home?

Little did I realize the Lord was just about to reveal the answer.

****

The next morning we woke to the sun pouring into our new room tucked far away from the little guesthouse.

Emma went in to take a shower as I snuggled in bed with our little gem, whispering to her how much we loved her and rejoicing that not only were we all safe, Ruby was with us forever.

Deciding I should change her so we could go for breakfast, I took off the tee shirt she had slept in. The window overlooking the grounds was expansive and sunlight filled our room.

I had changed Ruby for weeks now, but it was always in a dimly lit room, whether at the orphanage or at the guesthouse. Never before had it been so bright as I slipped her white tee shirt over her head.

It was then that I spotted something! I bent over her to have a closer look. What in the world were they? I took off my glasses and leaned down toward Ruby's chest for an even closer look.

My mind was completely confused. There were marks across Ruby's chest!! My eyes squinted as my mind raced. What in the world were the scars on her chest from?

I studied them closely. Perfectly aligned, they were spaced at what appeared to be exacting places. And they were identical to each other.

Bewildered, I rubbed my fingers gently across them. Ruby had been with me non-stop for the last few days and even at the orphanage. Before I had official custody of her, Emma and I had been there nearly all her waking hours other than when the paperwork necessitated otherwise. The scars had not been visible to me at all.

I kept running my fingers over them, my mind deeply troubled.

Emma was showering as I anxiously sat bewildered. I was praying for wisdom as I waited for Emma to come out of the bathroom. When she finally opened the door, I called to her, "Emma! Emma! Come see this! Can you hurry, please? Come and tell me what you think."

Emma came right over and peering down I pointed to Ruby's chest. "What do you think they are?" I questioned. Emmy bent down toward the deep, identical marks on Ruby's chest and shook her head in disbelief, her mouth open, "Oh my goodness! What in the world? Mom, what do you think they are? How come we didn't see those before? Do you think they could be scars from her brain surgery at the missionary hospital?"

"It couldn't be," I hesitantly responded, "and to my knowledge they never touched her chest with any piece of equipment. Look at how perfectly placed they are! They look so intentional!"

We both stood staring at Ruby's scars, completely dumbfounded. They were so exacting! What was even more puzzling was that we hadn't seen them before. It had to be the Lord's perfect timing now to see them and no doubt, it helped that the sunlight poured into the room so brightly.

I began to pray. Scripture tells us in Psalm 25:14 "the Lord confides in those who respect Him." I knew He knew, so I asked, "What are the marks Lord?" Very clearly, without any waiting, He whispered.

It was then, that all the pieces of Rescuing Ruby fell into place. Thank you Lord! Thank you for warning me that this was going to be a battle like none other. Thank you for protecting us all. Thank you for rescuing our precious baby girl. Thank you for your powerful love for each of us! And thank you for whispering secrets to me.

After hearing His answer, I decided not to say anything to Emma or Dwight. I wanted to have the word from the Lord confirmed, but in my heart, knowing His whispers, I knew.

Since painful circumstances had driven us to leave the former guesthouse under the cover of darkness, we decided that it would be best, given the situation that we not venture out from our new surroundings unless we absolutely had to. We would stay put and only leave if the situation necessitated it.

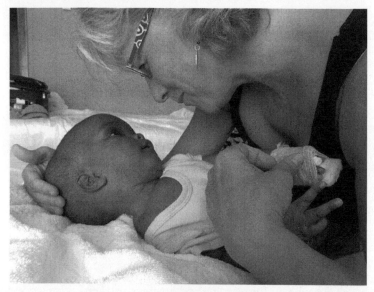

The day I discovered the scars...

****

One of the things we did have to do daily was to take Ruby to have her IV meds put in her port. This trip to the clinic gave us the opportunity to get a few things at a local store to eat and to visit with our new friend who was still a patient at the hospital. We were set.

A few days passed and one morning I woke feeling rather weak. A trip to the commode found that I was bleeding rather heavily from the rectum. I had never experienced anything like it before. I told Emma and she was adamant that we had better get to the hospital to get it checked out as soon as possible.

She definitely did not get any argument from me, as something was very wrong! Before we were able to head to the hospital I had been to the commode at least a dozen times, each time the results were the same.

After waiting our turn at the hospital I met with the doctor who quipped quite cheerily, "When you spend large amounts of time in Africa you are bound to get food poisoning! It's almost a 'right of passage' for those who spend time here. And my guess is that is what is causing all the bleeding." She ran tests and sure enough, she was right!

I was so grateful for the easy ability to figure out what was wrong - I did not need to be sick but rather I had to be at the top of my game in caring for our sweet little treasure.

Finally the US Embassy issued Ruby's VISA, our return flights were in place and the day arrived that it was finally time to head for home!

We had been living in Africa for seven and a half weeks! I smile as I think how Emma and I talked that final morning. Although we couldn't wait to get home, we also loved having this special time together. No matter how intense it had been, we had shared life in a way that could not be duplicated. I did mention to Emma that if she had not been here with me, Daddy would have opened the front door and found me on our front porch in the fetal position. I could not have done it without her!

Emma had prayed, fasted, cried, cheered, laughed, ran, talked, read the Bible, and persevered with me. She was not just my daughter but for several years she had been my trusted friend. We would never, ever forget the last seven and half weeks together. It held memories that we couldn't have planned for, wouldn't have dreamed of, and definitely wouldn't have thought possible.

We had many last minute things to tend to, but we could not leave the country without returning one last time to the place where Ruby had lived. Emma needed to see the little ones there and tell each of the precious little treasures she had spent so much time with just how much she loved them.

Hiring the driver that afternoon, I waited in the car with Ruby as Emma went in to say goodbye. After Ruby's last bout with yet another brain infection the last thing she needed was to pick up any other sickness. Her fontanel had been puffy and I knew the risk would be great if she were exposed to more potential germs.

I told Emma, if she should see Mama Naomi please tell her that we were in the car and we would love for her to come see us so we could say goodbye.

Within no time at all, Mama Naomi flew through the gate. She was so excited to see us! She threw her arms around my neck. I explained how we had not come around the orphanage because we could not risk Emma, Ruby or myself getting sick, as that would certainly jeopardize Ruby's health. I also mentioned that after I had gained custody of her, Ruby had yet another brain infection and been very, very ill.

In talking, Mama Naomi explained that she had thought we had probably already headed back to the United States. She was elated to be able to see Ruby one last time before we headed toward home. She had tenderly loved Ruby, gently praying over her and believing that God had good plans for her. We knew that God had definitely put Mama Naomi in that exact job at that exact time in history to truly be His hands and feet until we arrived.

With Ruby nestled in my arms sleeping, Mama Naomi and I were quietly catching up on life when suddenly I remembered the deep scars on Ruby's chest. Waiting till the opportunity presented itself, I lifted Ruby's sweet little dress and pointing to the very visible scars, I barely whispered, "Mama Naomi, tell me, do you know what these are?"

I will never forget the look in Mama Naomi's eyes as she heard my question and saw my fingers gently touching Ruby's very visible and perfectly aligned scars. Slowly she lowered her head, a profound sadness and shame overtook her as she barely whispered the words, "Witchcraft. Her birth family used her to perform sacrificial witchcraft rituals."

I felt like throwing up. Exactly what the Lord had told me was now confirmed. Witchcraft. Our precious gem from the heart of God had been used in sacrificial witchcraft rituals.

In rapid-fire succession, my whirling thoughts suddenly lined up perfectly and it all made complete sense. The warnings from the Lord before we even left the United States. Not just the fact that there was warfare but the intensity of the warfare was now understood. There had been obstacle after obstacle and the Chief Neurosurgeon's venomous words followed by the fancy (but very nasty) lady who had committed the heinous act toward Ruby. Then there had been the food poisonings and then the man grabbing me. Followed by another brain infection for Ruby and then the catastrophic events that left us running under the cover of darkness.

For those who don't understand, permit me to explain.

In Ephesians 6:12, it says: "For we wrestle not against flesh and blood, but against principalities, against powers, against the rulers of the darkness of this world, against spiritual wickedness in high places."

There is a very powerful spirit world around us and spiritual warfare is real. No doubt, the spirit world and the reality of it have been contorted and glamorized by movies that many well-meaning people dismiss as "fun". But the fact of the matter is that the spirit realm is at work around us. Jesus himself encountered the demonic on many occasions. Why would we ever think that the demonic world is obsolete today? On the contrary! It is very real and its efforts to thwart the works of Almighty God are deliberate, intentional and purposeful.

As we pulled away from the orphanage that day, we were reminded that it was the God of the Universe who had moved on Ruby's behalf. There had been so many opportunities for her to leave this world. From the significant disease that was attacking her brain, to the inability to keep large amounts of food down, to the fact that her birth family had given her to be used in sacrificial witchcraft rituals, to the abandonment in a garden under the intense African sun.

Yet, God had protected her life every moment of the way. Our Ruby had been treated with hatred, hostility and cruelty; victimized and made to experience fierce unconscionable and unimaginable pain, exposed to starvation for almost a full year, yet she had survived.

And as Ruby's birth family had planned their final monstrous act, the God of the Universe had been at work allowing their strategy for her demise under the blazing sun to be thwarted when a kindhearted soul would happen seemingly accidentally upon her and set into motion Ruby's ultimate rescue.

Of course on the opposite side of the world God had been moving on Ruby's behalf as Dwight and Emma planned the June

2011 GO Team for the exact dates necessary to find her in the corner crib.

In fact, Mama Naomi had said to me not long after we had arrived to complete her adoption, "God knew she would not make it, He brought your daughter and husband at just the right time to save her life."

Clearly, our loving God had placed Ruby where Emma, Dwight, and the team would find her. He had meticulously orchestrated each detail of her rescue so far. He would not leave her now.

Heading out of the orphanage gate that final day I was replaying the brief conversation Mama Naomi and I had about the scars and a shiver ran down my spine. We needed to quickly gather up our belongings to begin the journey toward the airport and I was more convinced than ever that our flight could not leave fast enough.

Chapter 12

"Let's Get Out of Here!"

Our driver had now become our friend and after leaving the orphanage that final day, he mentioned that he and his family lived nearby. He wondered if we would like to meet them. We were tickled to pieces as he turned the car off the paved road, winding over the bumpy dirt lane toward his home. After quite a distance, he pulled over and stopped in front of a quaint, meticulously kept home. He hurried on in front of us as we followed him toward the door.

His wife greeted us and happily welcomed us in. We were led into their living room where we all sat comfortably. She immediately insisted we eat something. It made us giggle. She fully intended us to have the complete African experience and loved every minute of their gracious hospitality.

In fact when we were leaving, our driver-turned-friend spoke, "From now on when you come to Africa, you will stay in our home." He had been such a blessing as we went from place to place getting the necessary documents to finally secure Ruby's long-awaited VISA to head home. It was such a pleasure to have both him and now his family in our lives.

He drove us back to the hotel where Ruby, Emma and I headed up to our room to pack the last of our things. Emma and I talked about how thankful we were that we had had so many weeks together in Africa. We had already loved the country, the culture and the people. The last seven and half weeks had only confirmed all that our hearts had already felt. Of course, since Emma would be eventually moving to Africa, if our stay had extended even longer, she probably would not have complained!

Piling our suitcases, Ruby's diaper bag and our carry-on items into the back of our driver's car, we headed toward the airport. When we reached the international airport, we went through security and then proceeded to the check-in counter. Taking our three passports, punching a few buttons on her keyboard and the woman behind the counter glanced up and commented, "I can issue you two your tickets, but I have no record of the baby flying." My mouth dropped open. "What do you mean you have no record of the baby flying?"

She continued, "There is no baby listed on your itinerary." What? I was dumbfounded. "Well I questioned my husband three times over the last few weeks and he assured me that he had spoken to the airlines each time and they clearly have our baby listed. Please check again." She looked down at her computer screen and punching a few buttons, she looked up and shaking her head side to side said, "Nope, nothing."

I was more than baffled! This was crazy! How could Dwight have checked not once, not twice, but three times and have the airlines assure him Ruby's ticket was there and now an airline employee was saying there was no record at all?

Always thankful for my African cell phone, I dialed Dwight. He couldn't believe it! He would call our friends, Gordon and Deb (who had graciously donated our tickets), and ask if they could figure out why it was not showing up in the system. Dwight and Gordon had been in touch the entire time we were in Africa and Gordon himself had also, weeks earlier, confirmed with the airlines that Ruby's ticket was secure.

I explained (again) to the airline employee that my husband had triple checked, our friend who had purchased the tickets in the first place had also checked...and all had said Ruby was all set. She turned the computer screen toward me and said, "See, you are listed and your daughter is listed but the baby is not." At that very moment, Ruby's African name popped up. I gasped, "Right there!" and as quickly as her name had appeared it was gone. I shook my head in disbelief! "It was just right there!" She had not seen it, or at least, she said she had not seen it. What in the world was going on here?

The once crowded terminal was thinning quickly. It was a midnight flight and most of the travelers had headed to the gate in anticipation of boarding. Emma and I were praying, but as the crowd disappeared I began to feel desperate. About that time we heard the boarding call for our plane.

And all the while, the airline was still not showing Ruby at all!! Finally, knowing that time was running out for the flight to board, over the phone Dwight said, "Just tell them you want to make a new reservation and book a new flight for Ruby." So I turned to the employee and said, "Okay, whatever. Just book me a new flight for the baby." She looked me in the eye and ever so slowly spoke, "We can't do that." "You what?" I asked.

Slowly, methodically and without any fluctuation in her voice she spoke, "We can't do that. Our printer is broken."

Now I knew what we were up against! The enemy who had worked so hard to keep Ruby in Africa was now stepping up every possible effort to deny her the right to leave.

I responded, "There must be some way for us to book a flight." She sighed, "You can go upstairs to the airline office and see what they can do." I responded, "But our flight is getting ready to leave." Looking back at her screen she casually spoke, "You're right, it's leaving shortly, you may not have time."

I ran as fast as I could up the stairs. I called Dwight and told him to PRAY! He knew that this was serious. Ruby's health had been deteriorating since her last brain infection and her fontanel was quite swollen. She needed to get to the United States now!

Once in the airline office, I produced my credit card and our passports. I explained the situation. The young woman echoed and elaborated on what the first employee had said, "The printers are down in Nairobi as well, we are not able to do anything to help you."

Oh my gracious! Lord, you have to do something! Nearly begging I questioned, "Please, can't you just hand write her ticket?" Shaking her head slowly side to side she answered, "No, we cannot do that."

There were two women in that office. One appeared to be a manager and the other a ticket agent. I pleaded even harder with them to do something! Anything! Finally they said, "You will have to call the airlines 800 number yourself to make the reservation." "But I don't have their number," I answered. The manager responded, "Call your husband and ask him to look it up." Seriously? They were taking Customer Service to an entirely different level!

I knew I did not have much airtime left on my pay-as-you-go cell phone but I quickly dialed Dwight again. "Please, the only way they are telling me to do this is to for you to call and make a new reservation for Ruby." In the meantime, our precious friends Gordon and Deb were on the phone with the airline as well, trying to straighten out the mess of Ruby's ticket and trying to understand how it could be there one minute and gone the next.

The airline manager brought a bit of hope when she said to me, "Maybe your husband will be able to make the new reservation fast enough. We will move you to the gate in hopes he can. If he can't you will have to leave the airport."

I followed her downstairs. The airline ticket counter employee downstairs led Emma, Ruby and I toward the gate.

I had almost forgotten that we had to pass the African Immigration officer sitting at his desk in his Immigration office. I handed him our two American passports and Ruby's African passport. He did not look too happy. Last time, leaving with two of our other children we had adopted, the man at the Immigration desk had not been very helpful. I was dreading talking this man.

This time the gentleman looked up at me and rather briskly spoke, "I will need to see her court ordered papers." I had prepared them ahead of time and pulled them out quickly and handed them to him. He looked them over carefully. Then he snapped, "Go make a copy of them for me." I responded, "They are boarding our flight, and I don't know where a copier is." He bristled and barked, "I said I want a copy!" "Oh! I didn't understand you. That is a copy sir! I made it for you. You can keep it." He slowly backed down and hesitantly allowed us to pass.

144

We went around to the security clearance. The airport was now empty. Passing through the x-ray system, we now stood waiting where the airline employee had told us to wait.

Emma and I were praying softly out loud. We could not believe this was happening! The airline employee who was standing at the door that leads to steps down to the outside and onto the tarmac looked sympathetically toward us. I went to her and spoke softly, explaining that Ruby's health was desperate, we must get on that flight and get her the medical help she so urgently needed.

As we stood there peering out in to the darkness, right in front of the massive windows was the aircraft we were to board. It was close enough that we could see the crew inside the cockpit. We could not tell if they were able to see us, but we could clearly see the captain and officers inside the cockpit.

Praying earnestly, pleading with the Lord and speaking powerful prayers of spiritual warfare, before long God's peace completely flooded my soul. My pleading now turned to praising Him. I had confidence He would rescue Ruby and complete her miraculous exit.

The manager came from out of nowhere and said, "We're closing the flight." With tears in my eyes I questioned, "Please, can we just wait another few minutes? My husband and our friend are both independently on with the airlines trying to make our baby's reservation." She shrugged her shoulders and almost excitedly quipped, "Nope! You can't."

Calmly I asked, "When is the next flight out? Can we go on that one?" This manager rolled her eyes and shrugging her shoulders she unenthusiastically responded, "I have no clue. You'll have to look yourself." Her lack of helpfulness was alarming to my soul.

With that exchange, the manager turned and walked away and I turned my attention back to the big glass windows. I whispered to Emma, "Do you think the crew can see us?" She wasn't sure.

Ruby's health was desperate. Emma and I prayed together quietly, "Lord stall the plane. Do whatever you need to do to keep them here."

In the meantime the woman standing guard at the door exiting the terminal to the plane was watching us. She seemed to take pity. About this time, a young male airline employee entered the waiting area. He had been loading the last of the bags leaving. Our bags were still beside us. She called to him, "Hey, this woman, her daughter and the baby really need to get on that flight. Can you help us bypass the need for a ticket?"

I giggle at it all. He was not a manager. He was not instructed by the manager, but God was moving on the hearts of a few of the people around and so the young man and the lady who once was standing guard now turned their attention to the computer screen nearby as together they tried to bypass the situation on the ground and produce the ability for Ruby to board.

Suddenly, out of nowhere, two men came running toward the security clearance. They were passengers and they were trying to make the waiting flight. Taking off their shoes, they glanced up at Emma, Ruby and myself. I called to them, "We are supposed to be on that flight and although my husband was assured by the airlines three times that our baby's flight was booked, they cannot find her reservation. So if you are so inclined to slowly move toward the plane, it sure would help us out!" They laughed. And they proceeded with the most dramatic slow motion moves in an exaggerated attempt to make the entire process slow to an almost stop. They demonstratively moved toward the door leading to the aircraft below and turning back, each gave us a knowing smile. Their kindness was heartwarming.

Time was past running out.

****

In the Old Testament when a new aspect of Jehovah God was made known to the Israelites they would add that characteristic to His name. When they needed provision, He would become known to the Israelites as Jehovah Jirah (God the Provider) and when they needed peace, He became known as Jehovah Shalom, when healing was needed, He made himself known as Jehovah Rapha and so on.

Dwight and I, many years ago, began to call Him "Jehovah of the Last Second" because so many times we would see God show up and move at the very last second.

Actually one time, with the adoption of Elijah and Elizabeth, we thought the last second had run out. But clearly it had not. And so we came to know Him as "Jehovah of Overtime" because we would marvel to each other and say, "Just when we think there is no last chance left, He still comes through in the overtime!"

****

I can remember standing with my eyes glued on the aircraft sitting directly in front of us on the tarmac and whispering, "Okay, Lord, I give this to you. She says it's closed. Your will be done. We are convinced we need to go on this flight. Ruby's health is deteriorating, but you know best. We submit to your will. And by the way Lord, if you want to be Jehovah of Overtime, we are all okay with that as well."

We stood waiting. Even though she had told us it was over, I could not leave and would not leave, until she clearly told us to get moving.

All of a sudden, over the loud speaker again we heard, "Flight 63 is calling for passenger So-n-So." Emma and I turned to stare at each other. Our eyes both grew wide! The Lord was hearing our prayers. They still had been unable to locate yet another one of their passengers.

The call for this passenger was again repeated. He appeared to have disappeared!

Minutes passed and then, ever so slowly, out of a lounge not far from where we were standing, moseyed a man, complete with turban piled high on his head. Clearly, he was not going to be rushed. Heck no!! In fact he looked at Emma and I with a twinkle in his eye and took his good ol' sweet time as he moved through the security check and clearance. He was actually moving (as my grandmother used to say) "slower than molasses in January!"

We could not help but smile. And down deep I wondered if he were an angel unaware sent to stall the plane yet a few more minutes.

I called Gordon and Dwight both. Finally! A new reservation had been made in Ruby's name. I ran to the woman and young man trying to work Ruby into the system and said, "Check, please! Her new reservation has been made!" Emma and I were filled with such hopeful expectance!

They refreshed the screen again and then again. Looking up they added, "Sometimes it takes 15 minutes to show up in our system." Oh my word!! Seriously?? It was almost laughable. How could a ticket bought over the Internet not show up immediately in their system? Who knows? But now we had a new glitch because, as they now said, sometimes it would take 15 minutes to appear in their system!

It was then that two young men, whom we had not ever seen before, appeared out of seemingly nowhere and lifting up our suitcases said, "We will take your bags to the aircraft. If you don't get the reservation we will have to pull them off, but at least they will be there." And they carried our bags off.

About that time, the young man working with the woman excitedly questioned loudly, "Did you get it? Did you get it?" He had somehow managed to rig past the system and then as fast as they said that, the woman said, "No! You did it wrong, that's not what we need!" I have no idea what they were doing, but they were desperately trying to help and we are forever grateful for their hearts that clearly cared that Ruby's medical situation was critical.

At that point the not-so-helpful manager showed up again and waving her hands in a "Go on! Get out of here!" motion exclaimed, "You need to leave, the flight is really closed." I explained that we had a completely new reservation now for Ruby! I further added that since the airline could not find the original one my husband had gone ahead and purchased a new one. While I spoke to her, out of the corner of my eye, I saw the woman and young man refreshing the screen over and over and over.

I peered toward the plane outside. We could see that there were actually people gathered out on the stairs smoking. I knew they could not back the enormous aircraft up without the group moving from the stairs, so I still didn't move either, but kindly said, "They're still on the stairs. They aren't moving yet."

She didn't argue the point. She just turned and sauntered away.

The Lord reminded of a scripture I had memorized many years ago. It has been applied to so many of my life's situations, "Those who hope in the Lord will not be disappointed." *He was our only hope. We just needed to relax and watch the rescue continue to unfold.*

Emmy, Ruby and I stood praising and thanking the Lord for His rescue, knowing it would come. He had always been faithful, would He ever even think of leaving us now? Had He fallen asleep? Had He quit caring? Not a chance! With all the opposition on every front, we knew that He would prevail, because when God writes a story, He makes it twist and turn with such anticipation that no one can ever say, "I did this!"

The word "ordinary" is not part of who He is, but rather if the most appropriate word to describe a story is "extraordinary" then, no doubt, it has His loving fingertips all over it. It is because of His most extraordinary and miraculous ways that He would be the only one who receives all the glory, honor and praise from Rescuing Ruby!

Minutes continued to pass. Finally it had been a full fifteen minutes since Dwight had made the reservation. Still nothing. That determined woman and young man refreshed that screen probably more than a hundred times. Yet there was nothing. All the while, Emma and I kept our eye on that plane. The crew appeared to actually be out on the steps as well. Odd. But we were so thankful. As long as the Lord was on the throne, and the aircraft was still there, there was complete hope that we would still get out of Africa tonight.

Over the loudspeaker a voice announced, "Flight 63 has closed its doors." The flight that was supposed to leave at 11:40pm had now waited almost a full hour. It was 12:36 am. As we heard those words we stared at the aircraft. A crewmember was in the cabin, but clearly, two men were out on the steps.

We did not move. We stood steadfast. Waiting. Trusting. Believing. Praising. He would do it still, no matter what the announcement said.

I had resolved in my heart that I would only move when the plane actually pulled away and was in the air. No one was forcing us to leave. So we waited. Quietly we whispered praises to His mighty and powerful name.

I moved over to the woman and young man and whispered, "Please try again." They did. Nothing.

Suddenly, out of nowhere, someone excitedly yelled, "Take them to the aircraft. Take them. Hurry! They are waiting. Hurry!! Run!"

We turned to see the original ticket agent that we first encountered when we had arrived at the airport hours earlier (who had said that she could not help) running into the secured area we were standing in. Believe it or not, she was actually waving a sticky note!! She thrust the sticky note at the woman who had been working with the young man and nearly shouting said, "This is the baby's ticket!!" (Yes, a sticky note. Not even kidding!) Turning to Emmy, Ruby and I, she yelled, "Go with her! Run! Ruuuuuunnn!!!"

Well let me tell you, we grabbed our carry-on and took off running at lightening speed. Glancing toward the plane, I could see it still sitting there.

As I ran I began to sweat. Not because of the run but because I was suddenly very concerned at what the pilot would say to us. The plane was clearly waiting because of our situation and I was dreading the thought of the pilot scolding us or yelling at us. I grew up in such pain, to this day; the little girl in me cannot stand to hear anyone yell. I actually began to get teary thinking that at a minimum the other passengers would be angry with us, let alone the man in charge of the entire flight.

Running across the tarmac, carrying Ruby I was wincing at the thought of what would greet us at the top of the stairs. Hurriedly we climbed the steps.

Reaching the last few stairs I glanced up to see three uniformed officers from the cabin and a bunch of flight attendants, all waiting for us out on the top deck of the stairs. Seriously, there were at least seven standing waiting as we arrived on the landing of the stairs. To our shock, there was not one scowling face. Every single one of them was smiling. Seriously. Every single one of them was smiling. Smiling!

As I took the necessary steps across the small landing toward the cabin door, I actually found that the Captain was standing on the landing to the right of the door, with his right hand outstretched to shake mine. I reached to his open hand and he clasped his left hand over my right hand. Both of his strong hands engulfing my hand as he said the most precious words beyond anything I could ever have imagined, **"It's okay! You're safe with us now!"**

My mind was reeling! "We were safe?" We wondered what he meant!

I apologized profusely for delaying the flight. With kindness this tenderhearted airline Captain repeatedly assured me, "It's okay. No problem. I want to talk to you later in the flight. **For now, let's just get out of here!"** Yes, the captain really said that! **"For now, let's just get out of here!"**

One of the male flight attendants led us to our seats. Walking through First Class we saw the two men who had stalled going through security. They smiled at us and gave us the thumbs up! I smiled at passengers as I passed through. Surprisingly, my smile was not met by one frown. All were pleasant looking and some smiled back.

As we neared the rear of the aircraft the flight attendant leading the way found that people had moved about in anticipation of takeoff and our seats were now filled. The plane was fairly full so it appeared that Emma and I could not sit near each other. But, on his own, this helpful flight attendant asked a few people if they would be willing to move and found Emmy and I seats together.

I could not reach Dwight so I quickly phoned Deb only long enough to say, "On the plane, by God's grace - call Dwight and tell him!"

We were literally airborne within moments of being seated and as quickly as the plane ascended into the sky, Emma, Ruby and I drifted off to sleep with Ruby nestled into my chest. No doubt, we were all wore out from the eventful evening!

A couple of hours into the flight I woke with a start. Ruby was fussing a bit and would need a bottle, so I woke Emma to hold Ruby while I headed to the back of the aircraft galley to find some water for her bottle. I was pretty groggy.

Asking one of the flight attendants for some hot water, I had not noticed that directly beside the flight attendant was the Captain (the kind man who had clasped my hand as we boarded.)

Turning to the Captain, the flight attendant declared, "Here she is!" The Captain had been looking for me because he wanted to find out what had been happening in the airport as they waited.

I shared what had happened. It was then that I learned what the Lord had been doing behind the scenes on precious Ruby's behalf!

Listen to this!!

A young woman flight attendant named Sarah was making a cabin check as most of the passengers had already boarded. She looked at her list. The cabin sheet said that there was a baby on the flight. She searched up and down the aisles. She could not find the baby even though one was listed. (Remember the airport staff had said that Ruby was not listed? Although for a split second I had also seen her name on the ticket agent's screen.)

After thoroughly looking through the aircraft she went to Jonathan, the attendant in charge of the flight. She asked if he had noticed where the baby was that was listed on the flight? He then did a thorough search. He could not find the baby either.

Jonathan then went to the captain of the aircraft and said, "There is supposed to be a baby on the flight, but we are unable to find her." Captain Graeme S. called the terminal and inquired,

"Do you have a baby that is supposed to be on the flight?"

The unhelpful manager responded, "We have a mom, daughter and baby, but the baby does not have a boarding pass." Captain S. told her, "Put them on the plane!" She then replied, "I can't, the baby doesn't have a boarding pass." To which this courageous and tenacious pilot demanded, "I don't care if the baby has a boarding pass or not, the baby is listed on our cabin sheet and is supposed to be on this flight! Put the baby on *now*!" She answered back, "I can't."

He firmly replied, **"I'm not leaving Africa until that baby is on this flight!"** And he proceeded to wait and wait and wait and wait. He called her several times demanding that she put the baby (and mom and sister) on but she repeatedly refused.

My mouth was gaping as I heard his side of the story! He had been defending and advocating for my Ruby without even knowing her situation. He had no clue that her medical needs were becoming more alarming each day, but God knew and was moving on her behalf through one very bold, determined and persevering pilot! After an hour the woman inside the terminal had realized Captain S. meant business and she had finally conceded making a sticky note-boarding pass for our miracle baby girl.

He then wanted all the information so he could report it to his superiors.

As I made my way back to our seats, I began to cry. Faithful God. He had had our back the entire time. He was making a way when there seemed to be no way! He was infuriating one heroic pilot, who didn't even know us, to move every single mountain and obstacle to rescue Ruby.

The battle had been fierce, but Almighty God had prevailed, using means that we didn't even know existed. How we praise His name!

When we arrived at Heathrow we slowly gathered our things. We knew we had an eight-hour layover so there was no point to rush. At about that time, Jonathan, the chief flight attendant said, "Oh wait! You have to take your bags with you." I was rather confused, so I asked him what he meant. He went on to tell us that the same airline manager at the airport had refused to load our bags because she said the aircraft was closed.

Captain S. told her to bring the bags to the stairs. His crew had carried our bags up to the aircraft and because of their size weren't sure what to do with them. They were clearly not carry-on. Captain S. told his crew, "Just store them in First Class". We laughed and laughed. Our well-missioned rather dilapidated bags were laid behind the seats and rode First Class the entire way from Africa to Heathrow!

But now we would have to figure out how to get them from this flight to our flight in eight hours. I whispered a prayer, "Lord, what are we going to do with them?" Literally, at that very moment, Jonathan, the director of the cabin crew, said, "I'll tell you what, we'll help you with your bags. Hey so-n-so, can you give me a hand?" Then turning to us, he continued on, "Just wait for us right here, we will walk with you and get your bags all checked in. You don't need to worry about anything."

For the next hour, the flight attendants of British Air Flight 63 walked with us through the terminal, on the tram and through the next terminal until we reached a place where our bags could be put on our next flight. I never had to lift a finger and neither did Emma. Of course our arms were already filled with our precious Ruby and all our carry-on items.

When we reached the place where we could get our next boarding pass and put our bags through, Jonathan actually asked for a manager. I realized what he was going to do and said that it was okay for him to leave, as he had already blessed us so much. But Jonathan insisted that he was not leaving and that he was going to be sure that British Air made it right! He told the manager, "These two women have been very poorly treated by the BA folks in Africa, could you do something for them?" The manager made a phone call and to our surprise, but delight, we were upgraded to First Class for our flight across the Atlantic. To think, that Ruby was going to arrive First Class!

There is no doubt that the verse in Isaiah 49:23 rings true: "Those who hope in the Lord will not ever be disappointed!!" God had truly rescued our sweet Ruby!

Chapter 13

Phoenix

After getting our suitcases stowed at Heathrow, Emma, Ruby and I settled in for a delicious full English breakfast. An eight-hour layover allowed us the opportunity to stretch out and relax some. In between little bottles of formula Ruby slept most of the time.

Every so often I would check her fontanel, which was bulging. Admittedly, I was fighting the ever-present urge to panick. The flights were long and with so much time being spent at altitudes that caused plastic containers to burst I just knew that this could not be helping all the fluid inside Ruby's sweet head.

Having finished eating, we spent time drinking several cups of coffee as we rehearsed the events of the flight out of Africa. We were in complete awe of how God had worked behind the scenes to use an airline pilot who knew absolutely zero of Ruby's situation. For those who doubt God's existence, the escape the night before would be pretty difficult to explain away! Only our powerful God could have caused Captain S. to have such a relentless determination!

Eventually we decided we should walk for a while. No doubt though, the departure time could not come quick enough. Getting Ruby back to the States and to the hospital was all that mattered.

I was so thankful that the Lord had whispered to fly out of Phoenix and I was equally grateful that our sweet pediatrician, Dr. Pakhi in Colorado, had researched extensively to find a competent, kindhearted and world-renowned pediatric neurosurgeon in Phoenix. Dr. Pakhi had taken the time to speak to this highly respected and extremely skilled neurosurgeon, Dr. David Shafron, at Phoenix Children's prior to Emma and I even leaving for Africa. After speaking to Dr. Shafron, our pediatrician was convinced that he would be the very best match for our newest treasure. Once we had met Dr. Shafron we knew that God's mighty hand had guided Dr. Pakhi in her search for a neurosurgeon.

Before we even left for Africa, Dr. Pakhi had spoke with Dr. Shafron and it was decided that Ruby would meet him at his office the day after we landed. But the entire process had taken weeks longer than we had expected and Dwight had had to call and change the date several times. After the fourth change, it was then determined that we would just take Ruby to the Emergency Room upon landing. Each time I looked at Ruby's fontanel, I knew that that was the very best idea possible and I also was

162

guessing that we would be not heading to Colorado any time soon.

As we talked of landing in America, Emma and I were so grateful that Dwight and the kids were driving to Phoenix to meet the plane. It had been seven and a half exhausting, stress-filled, long weeks since we had hugged our little treasures. We could not believe we had made it seven and a half weeks without being with them.

I mused to myself as we sat waiting for the last leg of our journey toward home remembering...

Days before leaving for Africa I had found myself questioning how I would endure being separated from my little ones. I detested the idea. I don't even really enjoy being gone from them to go grocery shopping! They are all my little sidekicks. I couldn't imagine doing life without them!

Of course, at the same time I desperately wanted Ruby home! Although I was pleading with the Lord that we could quickly swoop in, grab Ruby and dash toward home, I knew the reality of adoption. No matter how desperate anyone's medical situation, the process is always complicated by so many variables and circumstances that are entirely out of one's control. Even though I understood all that, I had emphatically told Dwight, "Okay babe, here's what we'll do. I'll go and get the process started, but you will have to come and relieve me. I am definitely not staying away for ages. I cannot be gone for very long."

Recalling my words, I shook my head and sighed. By God's infinite grace and mercy, the seven and a half weeks, although extremely difficult, were not only over but we had succeeded. Ruby was on her way home. The mission had been accomplished. The most precious little treasure in the world had not only been rescued, she was really ours and our precious pile had fared surprisingly well without me. No doubt, the power of many prayers whispered from around the world as friends prayed us to Africa and back!

Finally, in just hours, we would all be joyfully hugging necks and Ruby would be meeting the siblings who had patiently waited, fiercely prayed and lovingly longed for her for months now!! Just the idea made me want to burst!

As the departure time for Phoenix approached, our flight was called to board for the very last leg of our journey home. We were very honored to be seated in the unexpected, yet wonderfully luxurious First Class. What a delight we were gifted without request! We actually had a menu to choose from! There were large, comfy chairs. Emma and I kept giggling. Who would've guessed we would have such regal treatment? Clearly, we considered it a tender little love touch from the Lord.

As we settled in for the flight to Phoenix, I found that although the chairs were roomy and plush, I couldn't sleep at all. Fueled by my mounting concern over Ruby's fontanel, I was driven to intercession. It appeared to be bulging even more. It was also visibly more taut then when we had left Africa the night before and now Ruby had begun to toss her head from side to side with force. I knew that this was Ruby's way of telling us that her head was hurting. She did it as we flew across the Atlantic so much that my arm actually was sore and eventually bruised.

I prayed with passion,

"Lord you kept Ruby alive through all that she has been exposed to. You preserved her life as she was cast down and left dying, emaciated and starving in the garden under the hot African sun. In your infinite knowledge, you orchestrated events that brought a gentle, loving and caring African man to the garden to find her at just the precise moment that she needed to be rescued.

Oh God, you alone deposited tender character qualities that would make the man who lived near the garden sensitive enough to lift sweet Ruby out of the ground.

You also gave the man the wisdom to take her to the police station. You then worked through the police directing which orphanage she should be taken to - the very orphanage where Emma and Dwight would volunteer at just two weeks later and discover her on the very first day there!

Five minutes here or five minutes there and things would not have been the same at all.

If…if the man had not been walking into the garden that day…if the police had taken her to a different orphanage…if Emma and Dwight and the team had not scheduled the trip for the precise time Ruby needed them there.

Every thing would have changed drastically with any one of a dozen variables - yet you are the God of details.

No doubt, God, you have been watching and grieving over all that our sweet Ruby has been through, and your powerful and mighty hand has rescued her because your plans for our Ruby are good. In fact, your plans are so very, very, very good!

Surely, one of your plans, Lord, is to use Ruby's life to demonstrate to the world the extent of your love for a dying, abused, six pound, 13 month old orphan in a developing nation. Your plans are to work in her life and to work through her life. I'm even guessing that your plans are actually remarkable and magnificent for our little Ruby!! I just know that her life is going to touch thousands or even millions.

Oh Lord - you alone have faithfully protected Ruby each step of her rescue. I just can't believe you have brought her this far to have something happen at 38,000 feet. Nope. I don't believe it at all.

Thank you Lord for continuing your work in her life. You clearly have an amazingly beautiful plan for this precious treasure.

See your plan through, Lord; see that your plan is accomplished. I am reminded, yet again, that your word says, 'those who hope in you will not be disappointed.' My hope is in you and only you. Protect her brain. Decrease the fluid with your own hands. Minister to her frail little being. You are Jehovah Rapha, the God who heals. Do what needs to be done inside her head. Continue in the precise way you have faithfully been preserving her tiny little being to this moment."

I felt peace when I finished praying.

He had this.

The rescuing of Ruby shows Almighty God's loving fingertips were all over her life for a specific purpose! There was no way He would fail her now. He would complete what He set out to accomplish. My job was to trust Him knowing that He had been working and wouldn't quit just because we were headed to America.

Her story would be told to the world and He would get all the honor, all the praise and all the glory. He had taken care of so many details already, He was not sleeping nor had He turned His back, but, instead had gone before and the rest of the story was already being written by Him.

My spirit settled. I could rest in Him.

As we landed in Phoenix, both Emma and I were giddy. Finally! Finally! Finally! Although I could not wait to see that very handsome husband and all my treasures, I was not about to meet them all shabby from long days of international travel. I had tucked away a sundress, as had Emma, and after processing through Immigration with Ruby, and securing our luggage, we headed to the nearest ladies room to primp a bit.

Dwight later said he thought we must have missed our flight because it had taken so long for us to appear.

Walking through the Phoenix Sky Harbor international flight door to our waiting family was one of the sweetest feelings ever. A blur of squealing, clapping, cheering mixed with the running of little feet toward us. Our eyes were welling with tears. Reunited after seven and a half weeks. Such relief.

Ruby had been rescued.

Mission fully and completely accomplished.

Dwight had brought beautiful flowers to welcome us home. After all, it is not every day one gains another precious treasure!

Our dear friends, Dane and Laura and two of their sons were there to welcome us as well. It was so good to see their celebrating faces! Dane and Laura had moved to Phoenix the month before Emma and I had left for Africa.

Being some of our closest friends, when they had told us that they were moving to Phoenix, we had been so distraught. They had always been the type of friends who lovingly opened their home to our ever-growing pile of treasures, blessing us with love, acceptance, friendship and laughter.

Surprisingly, a day or two before they had moved, Laura had hugged me in front of our Colorado home and whispered, "I think you will be joining us in Phoenix soon." Through tears I shook my head, "No, I don't think so. One day, yes, that is our dream, but not soon." She shook her head up and down in complete confidence, "No, it's going to be soon. I just know it."

I never, even slightly, suspected how prophetic Laura's words would be, although they were spoken right in the time frame of the Lord's whispers to enjoy the view because I wouldn't be seeing it again. I just hadn't put it all together!

Josh, whom Emma was dating at the time, also had come to surprise Emma. Such joy everywhere!

Dwight, Graham, Liberty, Jubilee, Isaiah, Elizabeth, Elijah, Josh, Emma, Dane, Laura, Luke and Sam were all talking, laughing, oohing and aahing over our newest teeny-tiny treasure. It was such a beautiful time for our very weary souls to bask in.

We knew that the Emergency Room would be our next stop, so we all decided to head to the Chili's restaurant on the airport concourse. Seated around the table we told the story of Ruby's last official rescue when the courageous Captain S. announced emphatically that his plane was not leaving Africa "until that woman and her baby are on board." All of us rejoiced how God's plan had been accomplished through a total stranger, who knew nothing of Ruby's desperate and very imminent medical needs.

Each of my treasures made the rounds (well except for Graham and Liberty although they probably would have if they could have - ha!) to spend time sitting on my lap and snuggling with me. I was realizing that although I had landed, I likely would not be around for a while.

Daddy held his daughter. No doubt, Ruby clearly remembered the familiar song that he had sung dozens (if not hundreds) of times a few months earlier because the moment he began, "Oh how I love Jesus…" her tiny little body completely relaxed.

Ruby was safe.

Ruby was wanted.

Ruby was needed.

Ruby would now hear her daddy sing to her almost daily.

Ruby would be protected.

Ruby would be cheered!

Ruby would be snuggled.

Ruby would be carried lovingly.

Ruby would never know starvation again.

She would never lie alone in the hot sun in a garden.

She would never be abused again.

She would never know the private trauma of horrific deeds again.

She would never know the pangs of starvation.

She would never be left with her needs unmet.

She was now home with her forever family and her life and ours would never be the same again.

Ruby was now part of a forever family engulfed among six sisters and four brothers - seven of whom were also lovingly gathered from around the world.

And actually none of us knew that Ruby would not be the last of our treasures or that more would be heading our way before long. (Although to be quite honest, my heart always, always, always will hope and pray for more!)

She was now home with her forever family and her life and ours would never be the same again.

After a time of great celebration, we hugged Dane and Laura and their two sons goodbye as we all headed our separate ways.

As the Lord would have it, one of our lifelong and very dearest of friends is a neurologist in Phoenix. We stayed at his home anytime we were in the area, as he would also stay with us over the years. We had enjoyed many holidays and short vacations together as well over the years.

Learning we would be heading out of the country, Stuart had generously and graciously, once again, opened his home to our family. Emma and I had stayed with him as we headed to Africa to get Ruby. Now, that we had landed, he welcomed us all! Of course, I would be staying at the hospital with Ruby.

After leaving the airport, we took our children to Stuart's home and dropped them off so Dwight could take Ruby and I to

the Phoenix Children's Hospital Emergency Room. No surprise
that strong emotions overtook me as I carried Ruby into Phoenix
Children's Hospital that night.

We were here.
Finally.
We had made it.
She was alive.
She was safe.
She was home!

My entire being filled with sweet relief.

I reminded myself of something I had been thinking about
while in Africa. While knowing that an extended hospital stay
was likely, I had already vowed to myself that every medical
person who came in contact with Ruby needed to hear her story.
In my mind, there would be no exceptions. I would not only tell
them her story, but I would show them her picture too. That first
picture I ever saw of Emma holding our beautiful baby girl.

Truly, most people in America have never seen a person who
is dying of starvation. The vast majority of people in the Western
World have never worked in an orphanage on the opposite side
of the world.

For most, an orphan is usually a concept instead of a very real human being who bears a name, a face, a personality and many beautiful character qualities. To many, this abstract concept is shrugged off with the thought of, "Doesn't affect me so who really cares?"

Truly, in our luxurious world, at any given moment we can open our pantry or refrigerator and grab something for our taste buds to enjoy. If we can't find what our tummies are craving, we can head to a nearby store and usually purchase it.

Not so for the orphan. Even those deemed blessed to end up in a 'good' orphanage are often hungry. Food is scarce. When there is food, it is usually the same food over and over and over and over. Snacks are virtually nonexistent.

Most of our treasures were adopted as older children. Some remember vividly chewing on rocks to curb their hunger.

Yet I think about how many times as a kid I would grumble that my mom was serving leftovers. (Of course, now as a mom, leftovers are my best friends!)

I am convinced that if the bulk of people in our western world really saw an orphan up close or volunteered at an orphanage or hung out with some of the children that live on the streets in cities around the world, most would feel compelled to do something, anything.

They would see their faces. They would learn their names. They would hear their voices. Forever influenced by the plight of the orphan.

An orphan's life is usually not very pretty, yet most often their joy is undeniable. Something we in the West could really learn from.

I remember serving as a family many years ago at an orphanage in Mexico. Our Graham, who was about 12 at the time remarked, "Mom, isn't it weird that kids in America have everything, yet no one is happy? But kids in the orphanage have nothing and they are so joyful?"

Most when confronted with the reality of the orphan's life would cringe and they would be compelled to do something!

Anyone with a heart beating inside their body would find their "normal" completely undone and be driven to open their hearts, their lives and their resources to meeting the needs of these precious and largely forgotten treasures.

So my mind had been made up while I was still in Africa!! With our arrival at the Emergency Room and from there on out, I would keep the first picture of Emma holding Ruby's dying body near me so I would be able to share it with each person we came in contact with.

In an age of cynicism, filled with skepticism and unbelief, everyone should have the privilege of meeting a true miracle. Everyone should experience the joy of knowing the truth of how Almighty God had moved and orchestrated each situation to completely rescue our Ruby. They would not be able to walk away the same.

God would always get every single ounce of the credit. He would receive all the glory. We just had the privilege of having front row seats to this amazing miracle story!! But all would be certain to understand that it is only God who gets the praise, the honor, and the glory for Rescuing Ruby.

Chapter 14

It Could Implode

Upon telling the ER personnel that Ruby had already been diagnosed with Hydrocephalus, we were immediately whisked into an examining room. Once there we explained that we had been told to come right to the ER by Dr. Shafron's office.

Of course there was paperwork and tons of questions that needed answering before any exam could even begin. There would be a battery of every imaginable test - after all Ruby's fragile health situation was virtually unheard of.

A steady stream of doctors came in that first night just to take a peek at our baby girl who had survived against all odds. In keeping with my personal vow to show each person entering her room, her first picture, I began.

I wanted each medical professional, whether Doctor, Resident, Intern, Nurse, Physician's Assistant, Nursing Assistant, Surgeon, Technician or Clinician to understand that Ruby had been severely abused and the only care that would be permitted would be the most tender possible.

Each person was fascinated as I showed them her "before" picture and each appeared to truly marvel that she was alive! Albeit rather itty-bitty, she was now a whooping 11-pound bundle, for her 17 months of age!

The kindhearted ER doctor who spent the most time asking questions was truly intrigued by Ruby's story. He seemed to soak in every word. Sobered, he listened intently. Suddenly I remembered her scars. I had thought as we were flying across the ocean that I would need to notify immediately the hospital staff so that they could put it in her records. I would never want someone, down the road, to notice the scars and question where they had come from.

So literally, within an hour or two of being in the ER I told this attentive doctor about them and lifting her shirt I showed him. He was completely overcome with strong emotions and had to leave her room immediately. He did not reappear for quite some time.

It is unconscionable to fathom that someone who was meant to care, love and protect their own offspring would do the complete opposite and subject their vulnerable, weakened and tragically frail body to even more cruel searing, burning and pain.

Ruby's story was already having an impact. We knew it would. We didn't bring her home for that reason. Not at all.

We brought her because we loved her and wanted her to be safe. Yet, God had a much bigger plan in rescuing her. We were just beginning to see how much her life would influence others.

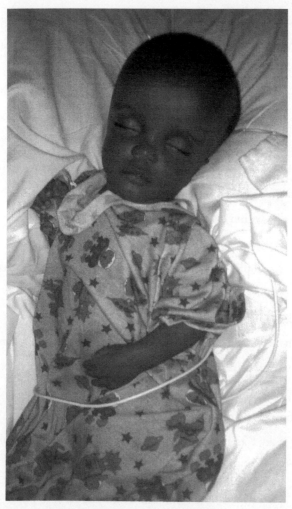

The night Ruby arrived at the ER in Phoenix...

I remember falling sound asleep off and on while sitting up on the examining table while holding Ruby as a steady stream of Doctors, Technicians, Nurses, Dietitians and Surgeons came to our little examining room.

It was close to morning when we were finally taken upstairs to her room. When we reached her room I found a metal hospital crib and commented to the nurse, "Am I allowed to get in that with her or could you possibly bring a bed that would allow her to sleep with me?"

The nurse enthusiastically agreed to have a bed brought so Ruby and I could snuggle together during her stay. I was so relieved. Ruby had suffered enough trauma in the last 18 months and I wanted to be sure that she was swaddled in the tender love, protection and safety of her mommy from here on out.

As it approached morning Ruby and I were finally settled together in her bed in a room at Phoenix Children's where we would be allowed to sleep peacefully for a bit.

The next few days brought more procedures than I ever knew existed. Her tiny spider-like veins continued to complicate every blood draw she needed. It was agony for this mama to watch them attempt to get a needle of any sort in them.

On Monday Dr. Shafron came to meet the three of us. From the second he stepped into the room we loved him! He was warm, kind, knowledgeable, skilled and very gentle.

After we spent some time talking, Dr. Shafron asked us to come outside her room so he could show us on the lit screen what her MRI looked like. He tried gently to tell us that as far as the MRI looked, her brain was not visible. He didn't understand at first, that we already knew that.

I explained that I understood much from seeing the films in Africa. I sensed he still wasn't sure I really understood what he was saying. We assured him that Ruby was our treasure. No matter what. We knew that we had a gigantic God who had spared her life and we were sure He had an amazing plan for her. We were smitten and we would do anything to make her know that we were over-the-moon in love with her.

No matter what.

He then understood.

He then went on to say that Ruby would need to live near a major neurosurgical center because her life was fragile and things medically speaking could change in a second. He said we didn't have to choose to live in Phoenix, but he knew that our little town would no longer be a safe place to live given Ruby's fragile medical state.

I told him that Dr. John at the missionary hospital in Africa had told me the same thing and I had already told Dwight that over the phone from Africa.

But at that time, Dwight had told me that he just wanted to hear with his own ears from the doctor in Phoenix as well. And here, without us even questioning that, Dr. Shafron had brought it up and told us on his own.

Dwight and I looked at each other and without hesitation agreed, Dwight would go back to the church we had pastored for 7-1/2 years and resign as soon as Ruby's health was stable. He would then pack up our things and move our family to Phoenix.

Done deal.

It was only then that I remembered what the Lord had whispered to me just days before leaving to bring Ruby home, "Enjoy the view as you won't be seeing it anymore."

Now it made complete sense!

No wonder I could never picture Ruby in our beautiful home in Colorado! And as much as I had been frustrated that Dwight had never put Ruby's crib up while I was in Africa, it was such a relief to me now that he would have one less thing to do when he went back to our church to resign and pack up our home.

It makes me giggle as I type this chapter. Ruby has been home now for 3-1/2 years and she has never, not even once for one second spent any time in a crib. Instead it was lovingly passed on to our Autumn for her first child and our 7th grand treasure - Miss Everlly Rain.

Dr. Shafron said that he would need some time to think what the surgical treatment plan for Ruby should be.

Most people with Hydrocephalus have one place with water in their brain. Rarely some have two. It is extremely rare to have more than two. Dr. Shafron invited me to count with him just how many cysts filled with water we could find on Ruby's MRI.

Slowly Dr. Shafron and I counted all that we could easily see and together reached 12; twelve places of water to bring the rare diagnosis of Multiloculated Hydrocephalus.

A few days later Dr. Shafron decided, after much careful thought, that he would begin her first brain surgery and 'fenestrate' some of the water-filled cysts in an effort to have them 'communicate' with each other. "Communicating" actually means that the water between the cysts would now move freely about, enabling it to reach the soon to be placed shunt. This was exactly what Dr. John had done at the missionary hospital in Africa.

In fact when I told Dr. Shafron about the missionary hospital he got very excited and questioned me further. He explained that a neurosurgeon who he had heard speak at conferences had started this very missionary hospital! He went on to say that this very hospital was on the forefront of Hydrocephalus treatment for the entire world!!

We could hardly believe it! Ruby had had her first brain surgery at the very place that was leading the way in Hydrocephalus treatment! The wonderment of it all - the God of the Universe had been moving on Ruby's behalf long before she had ever even been born!

In the following days many more specialists would visit her room. And true to my conviction, each would see the first pictures I had ever seen of Ruby. I wanted to be sure they appreciated her tender little being and understand why we were advocating for extremely gentle care for her!

****

One of the specialists who came in was an eye specialist. He had been requested to evaluate her sight. I had gone to spend some time with our sweet pile of treasures and Dwight was at the hospital alone with Ruby.

When I returned a couple of hours later, I could tell by Dwight's face that something was wrong. "What is it babe?" Slowly his eyes filled with tears, "The eye specialist ran tests on Ruby. He said she has Cortical Blindness."

"Blind? How could she be blind? She looks at us each day!?"

"No, her eyes roll around her head. She doesn't focus. Her pupils don't change size with the bright light in them. He said it is white behind her eyes, meaning they aren't getting blood flow and they probably haven't gotten blood flow in a really long time."

"What can they do about it?"

"There is a very slight chance that when brain surgeries are complete that the pressure from all the water in the brain will actually alleviate the pressure and she will gain some sight back. But he said it's a really, really, really long shot."

We were dumbfounded.

We cried buckets of tears.

Personally my greatest struggle with the news of Ruby's Cortical Blindness was that Ruby had likely seen those who had caused her such tremendous abuse, heartache and pain. I didn't want their faces to be the memory she held for the rest of her life. Purely selfish - I wanted her to see the family that loved her so very much!

In the days ahead we would lay hands on her, pray and then fast for Ruby's sight to be healed.

****

Ruby's first surgery was scheduled. It was so hard to deny her food as she waited for surgery. She had starved for so long that I felt like the cruelest woman in the universe.

After kissing her sweet little face and entrusting her to Dr. Shafron and his surgical team, Dwight and I sat in the waiting room, eyes fixed on the surgical door.

Each time the surgery door would open Dwight and I would hold our breath and wait to see if it was Dr. Shafron. Many times the door opened, yet it was not Dr. Shafron. When he finally did come through the door, we studied his face for any hint of what news he would bring from the Operating Room.

Our hearts were so relieved when he came through the door and waved his hands a bit and smiled ever so slightly. It had gone well, all things considered. Ruby had done amazing.

After surgery Dr. Shafron came to her room in the Pediatric Intensive Care Unit (PICU) to make sure her bed was set at just the right level and the perfect tilt to allow her brain to drain slowly and to keep it all functioning within extremely precise and cautious parameters. The attention to detail in the recovery process astounded me. Each of Ruby's needs were met with fastidious care.

It was after Ruby's first brain surgery that Dr. Shafron said to me, "I'm going to be honest. After Ruby had arrived at the hospital and I saw her first MRI films, I had no idea what I was going to do. I needed time to just think."

We deeply appreciated Dr. Shafron's humility. He had to think and weigh the possibilities and risks as well as the options. What integrity!

Within a few days of her first surgery, Ruby's second surgery was scheduled. Dr. Shafron would go back in and fenestrate some more of the many water-filled cysts.

From the onset of meeting with Dr. Shafron, he had explained in great detail that one of the largest threats to Ruby's life would be if the fluid were removed too quickly from Ruby's brain. If it drained too fast, her brain could actually implode causing her to die.

We felt sick if we thought about it. Ruby's life was so very fragile.

I write a blog (PlaceCalledSimplicity.com) that I have been writing for several years. I share my heart about the joy of large families, the blessing of adoption, the plight of the orphan crisis and always the faithfulness of God.

Many friends from around the world stop by regularly to check in on our family. Thousands have followed Ruby's story and I am so thankful for the privilege of sharing our family and the joy of Ruby's miraculous story on a daily basis.

****

I shared regarding Ruby's second surgery at PCH in the *following blog entries*:

November 19, 2011

Ruby's Second Surgery

Ruby's surgery went well

BUT there was a problem and

Ruby lost a lot of fluid in the brain and with that there can be great risks. The next 48 hours are crucial.

Thank you for standing with us in prayer.

We are thankful that Almighty God never slumbers or sleeps.

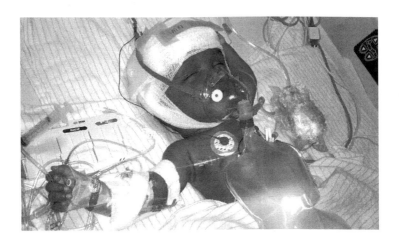

November 20, 2011

Concerns for Ruby

I keep starting, deleting, typing and retyping...all the medical stuff is just too hard to explain.

Suffice it to say that there were complications in yesterday's surgery. When we got up to her room Ruby was already there and doctors, nurses, surgeons and an anesthesiologist surrounded her. They had far more equipment hooked to her and around her then we had ever seen in her room before.

The complications would make it necessary to monitor Ruby closely. After several hours Dwight left to go to be with our other kids at Stuart's home and I settled in at Ruby's tiny feet, all curled up so she could feel mommy near.

I think I had slept for about 10 minutes and suddenly there was a commotion. Her heart rate was off the charts. The PICU doctor in charge came in. About that time Ruby had her first seizure. The doc immediately ordered a CT scan.

With the complications from the surgery yesterday, one of the very real dangers could be Ruby's brain imploding on itself or bleeding in the brain. (Hate even typing those words. In fact they make me want to throw up right here and now.)

I called Dwight immediately. A flurry of specialized medical professionals went into motion. Adrenalin was rushing through my veins and I was shaking uncontrollably as I stood watching. The PICU doctor in charge actually put her arm around me to comfort me as I bounced around from the rush of adrenalin.

We went for the CT scan. It showed what was suspected and the surgeon came right to the hospital.

By this time Dwight had arrived. They began giving Ruby a transfusion as she had now lot a lot of blood.

The surgeon adjusted the pressure in the shunt. They started an EEG that is still running. They started her on full strength oxygen. They tipped the bed in the opposite direction to elevate her legs.

Anyway, your specific prayers would be deeply appreciated.

Ruby's cysts/water needs to expand and fill the space.

Her heart rate needs to stabilize and return to "normal."*

Last night, when all of this was transpiring I stopped to text our older kids (Abi, Sarah, Autumn, Emma, Graham...).

Yet another beautiful thing about big families and grown up kids! They love their baby sister! Then I texted a few prayer warriors who I knew would pray.

****

Eventually, but rather late in the night, both Dwight and I posted on Facebook that the situation was serious and Ruby needed prayer.

I was so surprised how many were still awake and on Facebook in the States...immediately friends started praying...and precious friends in India (who have an orphanage) posted that they had gathered all the kids and explained the situation and wanted us to know that they were praying with the kids. Then my friend, Denie, who is a missionary in the Philippines posted that she was praying.... and people started saying what state they were praying from...very, very, very humbling to see the outpouring of support from (literally) around the world for our precious and once-orphaned baby girl named Ruby Grace.

Please don't stop.

And if you know any one who loves to pray - please share with them as well!

****

The potentially catastrophic consequences as a result of the sudden loss of so much fluid in Ruby's brain left us all visibly shaken. We knew that the only way her life would be spared would be with large doses of prayer. Fasting was in order as well.

Slowly the hours passed, Ruby's needs were tended to with precision, expertise and gentleness. Her whimpering was difficult to bear. It's one of those times where you can't think about it. I had to compartmentalize. She had already endured such pain!

Praying people around the world covered our precious little princess in prayer and just as God had been faithful in the African garden, His faithfulness was evidenced again, which served to confirm that God's plan for Ruby was bigger than we could dream.

Precious friends wrote Ruby's initials on their hands to remind them to pray!

As Ruby's PICU stay rolled into weeks there was a steady stream of medical personnel. Therapists, lab technicians, EEG technicians, nurses, MRI technicians, transport aids, cleaning aids, doctors, surgeons, med students, interns, Child Life caregivers, clinical specialists, pediatricians, nutritionists...basically, you name it, and they rotated through her room.

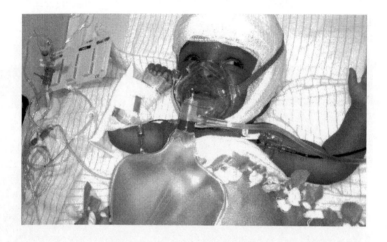

And my personal mission: Every single person who came through her door, would hear her story even if it was in the briefest form, see her "before" picture and then hear that God is a miraculous God! Ruby's story had Almighty God's loving fingerprints all over it and as long as I had breath, I would tell her story to everyone I encountered!

There was no denying, the God of the Universe had

miraculously spared Ruby for many specific purposes, one of which was that people would experience the reality of seeing a miracle up close! In this age of non-believers, doubters and skeptics, there was no denying the power of God - and to think - her journey was just beginning.

God had already done far too much for our littlest treasure to remain silent about His immeasurable love for her and the millions of orphans worldwide.

We had many friends come to visit while we were in the PICU. It was actually my birthday on a particularly not-so-good day for Ruby. I was shocked when blog friends, whom I had never met, came in a little stream and blessed me greatly!

One day, our longtime friends from Colorado, Jeff and Danica (who happen to pastor the Baptist church in the same town we were pastoring) were on their way through Arizona and wondered if we would be up for company and they were hoping to meet Ruby!

I had actually been praying for an opportunity to talk to Jeff and Danica as they were some of our closest friends in ministry. I never would have guessed that God would orchestrate their actually passing through so we could talk in person.

It was so good to see Jeff, Danica, Hannah and Micah! They each tenderly loved on our precious little miracle. After we spent some time visiting, we told them there was something we needed to share with them. We went on to share that we would be resigning from pastoring our church as Ruby's health necessitated moving to Phoenix to enable her to be close to her neurosurgeon. They were shocked! Later they told us they went to their car and sat and cried and cried. We are so grateful that they have been able to sneak to Phoenix every so often!

Eventually Ruby's health stabilized and Dr. Shafron decided it was time to put in the shunt. My eyes well with tears as I write., so much emotion and so many thoughts.

Thankfully, her shunt surgery went well and there were no big surprises or setbacks. As in the previous surgeries, her bed was adjusted perfectly and tilted at an exact angle. Dr. Shafron would come and check each time to make sure it was placed with precision to optimize her healing and keep the brain from the possibility of imploding or having any more traumas.

Dr. Shafron's fastidious care for our little treasure left an indelible impression on our hearts. He cared for her like she was his own daughter. Each time he came to check on her it was the highlight of our stay. He has a tremendous sense of humor, always kindhearted and a joy to know.

One day, after weeks in the PICU and three brain surgeries, Dr. Shafron came in to check on Ruby and told us that he and his family would be heading on a family vacation for the Thanksgiving holiday. He joked that he was thinking of packing Ruby in his suitcase to go along because he was going to miss her so! We giggled that he would care about our precious girl so much to tease of taking her.

But being perfectly honest, down deep I had to fight panic. He was the best of the best in our humble opinion, not only with his expertise in surgery but in his personal care of Ruby. I had to remind myself that it was the Lord who was her protector. I readily confess that I prayed hard for his family's flights and safety as they traveled - we needed him back safe and sound!

As Ruby continued to heal we knew that she would be moved to a step-down unit soon. Thanksgiving was approaching but she would still be hospitalized. About that time a patient advocate from Child Life, a program that makes your child's stay in the hospital more comfortable, came by to ask me a question.

She had heard we would be in the hospital for Thanksgiving and wondered if her Synagogue could bring a Thanksgiving meal for our family to enjoy in Ruby's room.

We were delighted!!

Here we were in an unfamiliar city wondering how we would celebrate our favorite holiday! What a joy to know that people we had never met were going to make it an unforgettable day!

Emma and I had talked and decided we needed to make it as much like home as possible. She would search and find some games and bring some cheese, crackers and fruit for snacking. We would watch football, snack, play games and eventually have our delicious Thanksgiving meal compliments of the Synagogue. It would be just like home, except in Ruby's hospital room.

As it turns out the day started with the gentlemen from the Synagogue arriving with their children and a pile of Thanksgiving meals, to be heated later. They were some of the kindest bunch ever and we had a wonderful time visiting with them. We were so grateful for their love and generosity!

Later, our friends Dane, Laura and their boys came up to visit. When we get together with them, there are always lots of sweet memories made. By evening our friends Steve, Cathy and their daughter came to hang out for a while as well. We had a blast with them. That hospital room was hopping and our day turned out to be one of our sweetest, most memorable Thanksgivings ever.

******

Ruby was released from the hospital about a week after Thanksgiving and we all went to stay at Stuart's home. Stuart's generosity was out-of-the-box as he had welcomed our large pile into his beautiful home from the time Ruby, Emma and I had landed. He loves our kids and is always so kind to them. In fact on the day of Ruby's first brain surgery, Stuart asked if we would mind if he bought the kids something fun. Turns out he bought a giant screen TV, an x-box and several games "to pass the time." What a thoughtful friend!

After Thanksgiving Dwight headed to Colorado to resign from the church we had pastored for 7-1/2 years. He would also begin to pack up our home.

We had lost our little log home to a fire in 2009. After the fire we had to live a hotel while we attempted to find a large enough rental for our family. After living in the rental for nearly a year, we had been able to move into a home we had just built not far from the spot our little log home had once stood.

It had been an emotionally exhausting journey - the fire, the loss, trying to inventory all the contents and then the rebuilding. Yet the thought of leaving our new home to relocate for Ruby was never even a blink on our radar. We loved Ruby. We would do anything for her.

When Dwight returned to Colorado to resign and pack up the house, Emma, Graham, Savannah all helped, as well as two precious friends, Danica and Megan. I am so thankful for their selfless friendship. Packing up the home of a large family is no easy task and even more so when Mom is in Arizona! Danica and Megan lightened the load tremendously and I am so grateful for their love for our family.

After quite a bit of searching we were able to find a rental home in Phoenix and Dwight and two friends drove the trucks down. It was such an exciting time! As an interesting side note, remember Laura's words as hugged me as she was moving to Phoenix, days before I left for Africa? She had whispered,

"You'll be in Phoenix soon, I just know it!" Amazingly, God provided a rental home in Laura's very neighborhood. Such a joy to our hearts!

Interestingly Dwight and I had always said that when we retired we would relocate to Phoenix. Finally, here we were at 56 and 52 "retiring" to Phoenix - only catch was that we had a medically fragile one year old and a pile of little treasures with us!!

Obviously, "retirement" is not on our radar and we couldn't be happier!

Chapter 15

Surgeries, Seizures, Signing and Seeing

Life slowly settled into a crazy new routine as the days and nights became a blur of caring for Ruby.

Because of Ruby's traumatic past, we already knew it was best to co-sleep with her... safe and cozy...cuddled against Mommy with the outside bedrail in place and Daddy on the opposite side of Mom.

Ruby had encountered such horrific, unspeakable abuse, starvation and brain traumas that we determined that Ruby constantly be made aware that she is safe, loved and wanted.

In January 2012, about five weeks after Ruby had been discharged from the hospital I noticed her more sleepy than usual. It wasn't a ton, but enough that I kept close watch. The next day she was just as sleepy. I joked with Dwight that, by the amazing grace of God, I was beginning to feel like I was becoming the Ruby-Whisperer. Yet in my jest, I was truly starting to think that something was definitely wrong.

By afternoon I called Dwight and told him we needed to take her in. Her life is so fragile, and must always be closely monitored! We couldn't risk a problem.

We were so thankful for the short drive to the hospital. Each visit, when the ER staff learns that Ruby has Hydrocephalus, she is quickly whisked back to a room because they know how deadly a problem Hydrocephalus can be in record time.

Although her last brain surgery had facilitated Ruby's shunt placement, suddenly something was very wrong!

Dr. Shafron ran an MRI and found that one of the previously fenestrated cysts had closed over, not allowing it to communicate with the shunt and this cyst was growing larger rather quickly!

I love when God works behind the scenes. We call God our Miracle-working, Mountain-moving, Awe-inspiring, Gasp-giving God because of the way He moves about carefully planning circumstances that we are not even aware of, so that when we have a specific need, He has already done all the "leg work" and all we have to do is stand and watch His miraculous love unfold before our eyes.

Sometimes His provision is so powerful we gasp! So it was that this particular time was a true "gasper"....

The last time we had seen Dr. Shafron, we were still in the hospital after the shunt surgery anticipating enjoying our first Phoenix Thanksgiving from Ruby's hospital bed. At that time,

Dr. Shafron mentioned that not only was he was headed to family for Thanksgiving but he had also mentioned that he was leaving in early December to attend a Hydrocephalus conference in Texas.

Unbeknownst to us, God was moving the circumstances just for our precious bundle!

As the Lord would have it, at the Hydrocephalus conference, Dr. Shafron had met a man who had a new machine that was being used to fenestrate the cyst walls in the brain. But the thing that was unique to this machine was that while it fenestrated each place, this machine would actually cauterize the new hole that had just been made! It was revolutionary!

Dr. Shafron actually told the man about Ruby and even commented, "I wish I had had this machine just a few weeks ago for this little baby girl I was operating on."

Now here we were, one month later, learning through tests that one of the previously fenestrated places had closed over allowing this cyst to no longer "communicate" with the other fenestrated cysts and, in fact, it was growing significantly larger.

Dr. Shafron also remarked that he couldn't believe I had noticed a problem. I gave all the credit to the Lord and said that the Lord had allowed me to earn a new title: "Ruby-Whisperer."

The decision was made quickly that Ruby would need yet another brain surgery. However, unbeknown to us, Dr. Shafron had located the man he had met with the new machine and found that, although he was based in California, he was currently in Ohio. Dr. Shafron asked if he would bring the machine to use in the surgery that Ruby would need immediately. The man agreed and jumped on the next flight bringing to Phoenix the new specialized equipment just for Ruby's surgery.

Again, my eyes well with tears as I type - oh how God loves His treasures!

As we waited for the man and his machine to arrive, we marveled over the lavish love of God for our little miracle girl!

In anticipation of the imminent surgery (and the arrival of the machine) Ruby had to be kept "NPO" - meaning she could not eat anything because of the upcoming surgery. It was during that wait that I witnessed an astounding miracle!

Remember the medical professionals in Africa had told the Director of the orphanage that there was no hope for Ruby? They even went so far as to say, "Don't waste your time on her. She will never do anything at all."

Well, since gaining custody of her I had decided that I would stand firm that Ruby was very much 'there', even if she didn't seem to be aware of anything. I was also fervently praying for God to show us that she was indeed aware and not only that, but that Miss Ruby actually wanted to chat with us, whether she had the ability to yet or not.

All day long we would talk to her like she understood us, believing that God was going to heal her.

Since I wanted to unlock her ability to communicate I had started, in Africa, to do three simple signs from American Sign Language with her. Many times a day I would take her hands and mimic the three signs. Over and over and over I did this, all in an effort for Ruby to understand that the signs communicated with us.

So that miracle day of her fifth brain surgery, as we waited without any food, suddenly, without warning and completely on her own, Ruby signed, "Hungry!" And she did not just sign it once!! Nope. She signed it over and over, "Hungry! Hungry! Hungry!"

Although I felt horrible that I couldn't give her any food, I was giddy. Ruby had just talked to me! She had told me she was hungry! It was one of the best days of my entire life!

Ruby was "in there", she wanted to communicate and she was clearly learning quickly! I had just started signing those three signs with her only three months before! And if that wasn't miracle enough, she had had several brain surgeries during the last three months that would have left the healthiest person woozy!! But our little treasure was not "woozy" at all, she was in there and she most certainly wanted to talk to us!!

To think that some thought she would never do anything. Obviously, they truly don't understand the miracle-drenched power of our lavishly, loving God!!

So that day, Dr. Shafron's plan was to do a sedated MRI prior to surgery and lay the images of the previous MRI over top of the current one. It was then that he would do a 3D trajectory image overlay and decide which way he would operate. Such a dear, caring, skilled surgeon taking his time for Ruby's best! An answer to so many prayers!!

After Ruby had been in the Operating Room for what seemed like forever, the waiting room door swung open. Dwight and I had been praying together, in the stillness of the empty waiting room, as the outside darkness had been seeping in.

We looked up, holding our breath. It was Dr. Shafron, but he did not have his normal smile on his face. Seeing our concerned faces, he waved his hands, gesturing in an "it's okay" kind of way.

He came to tell us that after the sedated MRI, they had moved sweet little Ruby, still under sedation, to the Operating Room and he had begun the surgery and opened her head.

Suddenly a piece of the scope had dropped below waist level. It hadn't touched the ground, it hadn't touched anything, yet he halted moving forward and told them to go get a new sterile scope.

When they had searched for a sterile scope they had learned that there was not one to be found in the entire Children's Hospital. Dr. Shafron then had sent someone to retrieve the closest sterile scope available - from another hospital! The surgery would be delayed.

204

Dr. Shafron mentioned that although he hated to have Ruby's head open and still under anesthesia as they waited, he didn't want us to worry. But the surgery would not be done in the time he had originally anticipated.

As he was turning to go back to the Operating Room to be with Ruby and wait continuing the surgery, I questioned, "Dr. Shafron, do you remember that I have a blog?"

He smiled as he nodded yes. (He had mentioned that he had peeked at it during Ruby's previous hospitalization.)

I continued, "Well there are a few thousand people around the world praying for you, Dr. Shafron, right now."

His face broke out in a humongous smile, "Really?"

Yup, really.

It was such a comfort to our souls to know so many around the world were kneeling together with us for our sweet Ruby.

The surgery went well, Dr. Shafron loved using the man's machine that had been rushed in from Ohio and although Ruby was fragile, she had done well.

Days later Ruby was released to head home to continue the healing process.

****

The next month brought Dwight and Emma leaving to lead a missions' team again to Africa.

It would be Dwight and Emma's first missions trip to Africa since Ruby came home and I admit I was a bit concerned about what would happen if Ruby needed to be hospitalized.

My fears were realized when, in the middle of the night and a week into their trip, I woke to Ruby beside me as her body's rhythmic seizing banged into my side. Oh how I hated to see our precious baby girl having this horrific grand mal seizure.

I called 9-1-1 and ran to wake up Graham. I told him to come quickly as he would need him to flag the ambulance down. Within minutes a First Response team, an EMT and an ambulance arrived.

When they entered our bedroom Ruby was still seizing and although they administered powerful drugs she continued seizing. The seizure lasted a full 30 minutes! When the EMTs felt she was stable they transported us to the nearest hospital, afraid to travel all the way to Children's.

While going into the hospital from the ambulance, she had another small seizure. Once inside, the ER staff took vitals, put in an IV and cared gently for her.

But suddenly she began to seize again. This time, the IV was in and they were able to administer a drug through the IV, however, the seizure didn't stop. Then they administered a different drug rectally. Still the seizure continued. The ER doctor then administered a third drug!

My eyes were glued on the pediatric ER doctor as I pleaded with the Lord for His healing power to stop this horrible second grand mal. Watching the ER physician in charge, I began to feel that she was starting to panic. This seizure, on top of the 30 minute one at home was wreaking havoc on our sweet Ruby and I know enough to know that any seizure that will not stop is life threatening!

The ER doctor was kind, compassionate and very competent. I knew she was doing all she could, but this unrelenting seizure would not stop. Three powerful drugs had now been administered and this seizure was not even remotely winding down.

With Dwight in Africa, and no way to reach him, I couldn't even think what to do. I then remembered my childhood friend, Dan. He is a mighty man of God who prays with powerful authority. Although it was the middle of the night I took my cell phone and ran to the hallway to call him. I almost screamed into the phone, "Dan, you have to pray!" Explaining briefly the situation, he instantly prayed with me and when I went back to her side, her seizure was ending.

All praise to the Lord!!

When Ruby was stable, we were transferred down to Children's Hospital and her neurologist came to see her. After we spent some time talking, I had to ask him his thoughts. I began, "The pediatric ER doctor at the hospital near our home was so very kind. She was gentle and caring. She was competent. But as Ruby's seizure refused to end, it seemed that she was maybe panicking. Could I have been reading her right?"

Ruby's neurologist looked me right in the eye and began, "I see seizures every day, it's what I do. But if it had been me, I would have been freaking out. Her seizures are life-threatening!"

Needless to say, it was a very sobering time and a gentle reminder that life with Ruby is fragile.

Ruby and I spent a few days in the hospital, as they wanted to keep a close watch over her and adjust her seizure meds. Just as I had suspected Graham did a superb job caring for his younger siblings. He planned some special activities and they loved the crazy fun!

When Ruby and I finally were able to come home I'm pretty sure the kids had not missed us one bit - thanks to Graham's loving heart towards his siblings that causes him to not only make each day special, but very memorable! No doubt, they each know, he deeply loves his younger sibs!

It was good to be home again and even though the events leading to her hospitalization had not been pleasant, I had the confidence, that even with Dwight and Emma in Africa, the Lord had provided everything we needed!

****

A few months later we had an eye appointment to establish an eye surgeon for Ruby.

Ruby's diagnosis of Cortical Blindness had come from the in-hospital eye surgeon after we had landed and every test imaginable was done to assess her overall health and wellbeing. Since that difficult diagnosis, we had been fervently praying as a family that God would heal Ruby's eyes.

What a difference a year makes...Emma holding Ruby

At that in-hospital exam it had been revealed that behind Ruby's eyes it was white. The hospital eye surgeon who had done the assessment and given the diagnosis of Cortical Blindness was very nice but definitely didn't offer hope for Ruby to ever gain her sight.

As it turned out, Dwight and Emma were once again in Africa leading a team when I took Ruby to meet the new eye surgeon who was supposed to care for her on an on-going basis.

Having not yet met this new eye surgeon, I was looking forward to what he would find. He had come with such rave reviews, that we were encouraged by several other parents that he was the one we "had to go to."

Immediately I found him to be rather abrupt and remarkably cold. I actually wondered how in the world he had gotten the rave reviews. In his defense, maybe he had just had a really horrible day, but what transpired next was downright mean, nasty and uncalled for, no matter what (if anything) had happened to him prior to him walking into our examining room.

It went like this:

Ruby's eyes were dilated. Upon inspection they were not dilated adequately so they dilated them again. Eventually we went into his examining office. When the doctor with the rave reviews came in, I was, of course, anticipating a pleasant visit (regardless of the exam results) based on the splendid reports I had heard from other moms about him.

However, he immediately looked at me and said, "Your daughter has Cortical Blindness and she will never see." It was so abrupt that I was kind of caught off-guard.

Smiling hesitantly, I remarked, "Well she was diagnosed with Cortical Blindness in the hospital when we first arrived from Africa, but we have been praying a ton and we believe God can heal her!"

He looked me square in the eye and without a change of facial expression, while completely ignoring what I had just said, he firmly responded, "Your daughter has Cortical Blindness and she will never see."

Not to be argumentative at all, but believing in the hope of healing that the Lord brings, I continued, "Well we really believe in the power of prayer and so I'm just wondering, what color is it behind her eyes?"

He answered, "Pale."

Excitedly I responded back, "See! We have been praying and God has been healing. It was white when she was in the hospital! If it's pale - that's better, right?"

He sounded irritated and again completely ignoring my question, he repeated the exact same words, "Your daughter has Cortical Blindness and she will never see."

Now call me crazy, but I am of the persuasion that there is always, always, always hope - unless maybe you've been dead for more than three days.

And in our case, we were counting on the ability of our powerful and mighty healing God! Because when we are trusting God, our hope becomes rooted in His supernatural, omnipotent power and things that everyone thought were once impossible, now become completely possible!!

Now not to have God's power questioned by Dr. Nasty, with every bit of graciousness I spoke softly and hesitantly,

"Okay, so please help me understand this. You're saying you think there is no medical way that Ruby will see? And you also think that God can't heal her. So would you be willing to say, that if Ruby does see one day, that you will give all credit to God, because it was not medically possible otherwise?"

Dr. Nasty turned and with an increasing sound of irritability in his voice, stuck his now reddened face toward mine and wagging his head minimally side-to-side emphatically answered me, "Your daughter has Cortical Blindness and she will NEVER see!"

For all my bravery, my eyes filled with tears as Ruby and I left his office that day.

Once in the car, I started to sob. What a nasty man, a true hope-stealer. Yet, the fact remained, Ruby's diagnosis was not limited to what a bully of an eye surgeon would say. No! On the contrary! Her situation had been and always would be at the mercy of God. And He loved Ruby immensely.

Crying as I drove down the 101 that day, the Lord and I had an important and lasting conversation. I gave Ruby's sight and future to the God who rescued Ruby and asked Him to continue to do the impossible!

I also mentioned to the Lord that it would be okay with me if He healed her eyes completely and I could have the thrill of one day taking our sweet little African princess to Dr. Nasty's office again to allow him to 'see' (pun intended) for himself just what Almighty God is not only willing, but more than capable of doing!

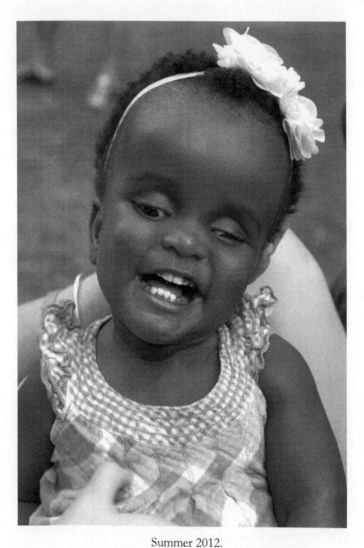

Summer 2012.

We drove across the country to see family.

Ruby did amazing! And that smile??

Just as miraculous as everything else!

Chapter 16

"Oh Really?
Now Watch This!"

After Ruby's two very significant seizures while Dwight was in Africa, we knew Ruby had much to overcome on her road to recovery.

A firm believer in baby wearing, Ruby spent her days being carried in my sling everywhere I went. Each day I spent whispering, talking, singing, and including Ruby. I was trying desperately to pull her out of herself. Many days she just wanted to sleep away and on those days she would have cool baths, sometimes three or four a day, in an effort to keep her awake.

Daily I was very concerned that if we didn't stimulate her, perhaps Ruby would not see a need to live and in that case, she could easily sleep away the rest of her life. Truly, we just couldn't bear that thought!

We needed Ruby to wake up and fight! We needed her to stay awake so she could realize that there was a big old beautiful world waiting for her to come out and play! Slowly, oh so very slowly, we began to notice teeny tiny accomplishments in our precious little treasure. These subtle advances, to the average onlooker, may have seemed barely noticeable, but we saw each as an enormous victory for Ruby.

Remember how we had been told she would never do anything at all? Each tiny triumph was a gigantic celebration to our souls! And every tiny accomplishment, we threw a party! And each itty-bitty gain, we cheered wildly! And every step of the way we had our hope spurred on by our Miracle-working, Mountain-moving, Awe-inspiring God, Gasp-giving God!

"Those who hope in the Lord will not be disappointed!"

Within six months of landing, sweet Ruby Grace was signing, on her own, three signs: "thirsty", "eat" and "friend".

What a miraculous discovery! Ruby could talk to us now!

****

Of course, knowing the power of prayer, we knew that the only one who was capable of the continued healing of Ruby was our gracious God who had lovingly spared her life.

One day, when she had been only home about five months, Dwight went to let our two little dogs out before the three of us headed to bed. After a few moments, Charlee Louise, Emma's dog, barked a few barks signaling she wanted to come back in the house. And just like every other night prior, turning to Ruby I questioned, "What does the dog say Ruby? Ruff! Ruff! Ruff!"

Except this particular night, immediately, with perfect clarity and much effort Ruby mimicked me, "Woof! Woof! Woof!" It was so distinct and there was absolutely no denying it. Thankfully Dwight had heard it as well and together we giggled, cheered and praised the Lord! Ruby had not only answered my question, but she had "woofed" three times.

****

Just as most of Ruby's early days were up and down there were definitely some days she would seem to be 'with us' and yet other days she seemed like she was locked inside herself. We continued to encourage her to 'come out and play' all day! We prayed daily that God would continue His healing work.

In fact when her physical therapist, Artemis, first came to evaluate her for therapy, Artemis made this observation, "Ruby has had such a traumatic and abusive past, and then endured five brain surgeries it would be impossible to imagine that she should be doing what someone else at almost two years old would be accomplishing. She has needed to recuperate from some major obstacles! We will have to just start counting her age from here!"

Artemis' words resonated in my heart and brought tears to my eyes. Her kind words gave us life-giving hope! No one could possibly think that she should pick up and be at the same place an average 22 month old would be at who had never experienced the tragedies, traumas and abuse that Ruby had endured. We clearly had to 'write off' the first 22 months - at a minimum! What comfort we found in that!

When Ruby had been home about seven months, Artemis, her physical therapist, began working with her. We were working diligently to stimulate Ruby and cheer her on, yet we were at a loss as to precisely how to work with Ruby in order to not only meet goals but to truly thrive!

With Artemis' help, we were able to set realistic goals for Ruby and each week that Artemis came to our home she would show us simple exercises and challenges to help Ruby meet her goals.

I would sign the word "friend" to Ruby and tell her that it was the day her friend Artemis was coming.

Ruby in her stander...learning to bear weight.
And seriously, that smile of hers!

It didn't take long till Ruby began to squeal with joy that her friend Artemis was about to arrive!

In November of 2012, one year almost to the day of Ruby's arrival home in the States, we had a remarkable conversation with our sweet Ruby...I wrote about it in a blog entry:

Our littlest princess continues to amaze everyone who knows her story...

Listen to this:

The other day we were able to head to our state fair…(Dwight found on the AZ Fair website that one specific day they allow anyone coming in between noon and 1:00pm to enter for free, how cool is that? A large family's dream! So off to the fair we went!)

We were barely inside the gates when the smells and sounds hit us....

There were thousands of people everywhere, talking, calling to each other, laughing and giggling.

I looked down and instantly Ruby started signing "friend".

I could not believe my eyes.

She was surely asking me, "Who are these people mom? Are they our friends? Where are we, Mom?"

Each Sunday as we prepare for church I explain to Ruby that we are going to church to worship and we will see our friends too! Clearly Ruby knew that we were not at church, but was, no doubt, wondering, "Who are these people?"

We were amazed!

I explained to Ruby that we were at the fair, and although there were many people and many *would be* friends, I really didn't know anyone to introduce her to. She continued to sign "friend."

I began to pray that we would see someone who would be able to talk to Ruby. I'm pretty sure she was saying, "Come on Mom! Grab some friends and tell them to talk to me!"

Within about 15 minutes of praying that prayer, I looked up and saw a woman from our church. The minute I saw her, I was thrilled and called to her, "Hi Sarah! Would you mind saying 'hello' to Ruby?"

Sarah was more than happy to do so and so I helped Ruby do the sign for "friend" and officially introduced Ruby to Sarah...and Ruby began to wiggle and smile and giggle. It was such a wonderful treat for all of us to see Ruby talking to her new 'friend'! And this mama's heart was rejoicing at the faithfulness of God - I mean, think about it, we barely know anyone in the entire state of Arizona - so to run into any one at the fair who could speak to Ruby - truly miraculous!

Some time later, as Dwight took the kids walking through the fair grounds, I was sitting on a bench and struck up a conversation with a sweet lady, who happened to have a son who also has Cerebral Palsy. I was able to introduce her to Ruby and little Miss Ruby was tickled to meet her as well.

There is no doubt that our Ruby loves people and the reality is that anyone who has the joy of meeting Ruby - loves her too!

****

No doubt, every one would agree Ruby's physical struggles are complex. Due to the Quadriplegic Cerebral Palsy, the Multiloculated Hydrocephalus and the size of Ruby's precious head, few believed that Ruby would ever be able to lift her head on her own.

Yet Artemis was working with her once a week, and we were supplementing each day, slowly attempting to teach Ruby how to tuck her knee under her body and give a little push which would enable her to roll over.

One day, when Ruby had been home about eight months, completely on her own, she tucked her leg all by herself and rolled! Oh the shouts of joy that echoed through our Phoenix neighborhood that day!

That first roll showed us something invaluable - Ruby wanted to be mobile as much as we wanted her to be!

We saw just what would happen when Ruby's dogged determination was coupled together with God's amazing grace.

But nothing took us quite by surprise as to what little Miss Ruby did next! About a month after accomplishing her first roll Ruby was about to do something astounding to all and it had only been a bit over a year since Ruby had come home.

As the Lord would graciously have it, our home was filled with some of our grown treasures and some precious friends to celebrate Thanksgiving 2012!

Thanksgiving's eve we were all crowded in our family room, some on couches but most sitting beside Ruby who was in her usual spot - laying smack dab in the center of the room on a quilt.

We were laughing and talking, loving being together...when suddenly, without any warning at all, Ruby rolled on to her tummy and lifted her very heavy head and looked straight ahead!

She then held her head perfectly still for about two seconds!

Lowering her head carefully to the floor, we wildly cheered and Ruby's entire body wiggled with glee, which made us all giggle and cheer even more! Hearing us shriek with delight, Ruby lifted her head again and held it perfectly steady while our cheers continued!

We marveled at how beautiful of the Lord to allow this enormous miracle to occur while nine of Ruby's siblings were gathered together to celebrate our most favorite holiday of all - Thanksgiving!

And just for some added emphasis Ruby did it again and again and then again!

Thanksgiving 2012 will forever be held as one of my most favorite Thanksgivings for many reasons: Our twelfth treasure Nehemiah had recently come home forever, our home had sold, Emma was home with us for the last year before moving to Africa, and our sweet Ruby was not only thriving, but she was making miraculous strides!!

How gasp-giving of the Lord to allow this enormous event to occur while so many of us were present to cheer her on!

****

By February of 2013 Ruby, the girl who we were told would never see rolled with purpose across the floor to stick her hand in a mason jar full of water! A clear mason jar full of crystal clear water! (Well as crystal clear as Phoenix water can be! Ha!)

Although I did not have my video on her to get that, I was able to capture footage of what she did next, which I posted on my YouTube channel. She wiggled her way over to the mug of tea on the floor and dumped it all over the rug. We giggled and cheered dreaming of the day we will return to Dr. Nasty's office to let him make a note for himself - Miss Ruby can see!

As the months would pass, Ruby learned her first word: "Guh-Guh" which she calls Graham. She adores her big brother and he thinks she's pretty special too. Guh-Guh was finishing his schooling the first two years after Ruby came home. Then he went to work full-time. The first days on his job she would say all day long, "Guh-Guh! Guh-Guh! Guh-Guh!" No doubt, she was not too happy that her big brother, who teased her all the time, was now gone each day.

In the spring of 2014, two and a half years after coming home, I was tucking Ruby into her side of our bed. I had turned on her monitor (which enables me to watch her until I crawl in beside her). Each night as I tuck her in I whisper how much we love her, pray with her and then finish by singing "Oh How I Love Jesus."

Oh How I Love Jesus is the song that, after Emma discovered Ruby in the orphanage, Dwight would spend any waking moment that he could, holding Ruby, attempting to feed her and always, always, always singing that song to her.

"Oh how I love Jesus, Oh how I love Jesus, Oh how I love Jesus, because He first loved me."

It's obvious that Ruby finds the song very comforting and soothing as we sing it.

This particular night in April of 2014 I had just finished singing "Oh How I Love Jesus" and turning to leave, I was stopped in my tracks.

What was that?

Whipping around I froze and waiting perfectly still the sweet sound continued.

What a miracle!!

Sweet Ruby was humming, all by herself,

"*Oh how I love Jesus,*
Oh how I love Jesus,
Oh how I love Jesus,
Because He first loved me.
There is a name I love to hear,
I love to sing His worth,
It sounds like music to my ears,
The sweetest name on earth."

I ran back over to her as tears fell from my eyes.

"You did it Ruby! You know how to sing Oh How I Love Jesus! You're a miracle! Every bit of you! What a perfect song to be your first! The very song Daddy used to sing to you when Emma found you!"

It was not only astounding that she hummed the song without any help, but equally astounding was that she hummed it with complete perfection. She had not missed a beat. Each tone measured precisely and every note on perfect pitch.

Since that monumental day, Ruby hums "Oh How I Love Jesus" so often that we have lost count. Such miraculous accomplishments for one who had once been deemed unworthy by medical professionals - even declaring, "Let her be. She's not worth saving, she'll never do anything".

By summer of 2014 Ruby had put her first two words together and decidedly declared when not very happy about the therapy she was doing, "All done! All done! All done!"

Lindsey, her caregiver, and I have laughed at how well and emphatically she has learned to say it, too! In the fall of 2014 we were at the doctor's office for our yearly visit. As the young assistant began to check Ruby's blood pressure, giant tears came rolling down her cheeks. Ruby rarely cries, almost never. It is so painful to watch as her mommy, knowing what she's gone through. Wishing it would all be over quickly, I hadn't paid attention to what Ruby was saying, until the young woman commented, "She's saying 'All done!'" I laughed! Yes she sure was! Apparently Miss Ruby had had quite enough of that dumb blood pressure cuff!

****

After humming, "Oh How I Love Jesus", Ruby began to add other songs quickly.

Learning some within hours of the first time hearing, Ruby has mastered the ability to hum alone, on perfect pitch:

Oh How I love Jesus

Itsy-Bitsy Spider

Head, Shoulders, Knees and Toes

Three Kind Mice (the new politically correct version)

Frere Jacques - which of course adds a bit of international flavor!

Always by Kristian Stanfill

Happy Birthday!

Jesus Loves Me

The Ants Go Marching

Oh How He Loves Us

Don't Go Breaking My Heart

You Are My Sunshine

My Favorite Things

■■

In September of 2014 I was working in the kitchen with our treasures when I remembered it was our Autumn's birthday. Excitedly I exclaimed, "Oh guys! Today is Autumn's birthday. Don't let me forget, we need to call her and sing Happy Birthday to her."

Lindsey, who was working on crafts with Ruby in the next room, explained that as Ruby heard me tell the kids that it was Autumn's birthday, Ruby instantly began to hum "Happy Birthday!"

I was dumbfounded. This meant, for starters, that Ruby was paying full attention to what was going on in the next room. She heard me tell the kids it was Autumn's birthday. She immediately knew what song was appropriate for us to call and sing. She wanted to be sure we knew too! Miracle after miracle after miracle!

In fall of 2013, Ruby was asked by the Central Arizona chapter of United Cerebral Palsy to be their Ambassador of the Year. I assumed it was a time for UCP to honor their employees. I did not understand it was a fundraiser for extremely wealthy people. Either way, we jumped at this rare opportunity! A camera crew even came to our home and filmed Ruby doing Physical Therapy with Artemis while also interviewing me.

All nine of our children who were currently living at home were invited as guests of UCP. There is no doubt that Ruby knew the night was all about her. She was squealing, smiling and clearly loving being UCP's Guest of Honor all dressed up in a dress given to her by her little boy friend Patrick.

After the dinner was finished, Ruby's movie clip was shown for all in attendance. In the video we had that first picture of Emma holding Ruby's dying body. There were not many dry eyes as the video ended and what a shock to see the entire room at the Ritz-Carlton rise to their feet and give Ruby a standing ovation! Ruby squealed with joy!

Sitting watching the evening unfold, I marveled to think that as Ruby was left to die under the hot African sun, not one person would have guessed that one day she would be the recipient of a full-house standing ovation by many of Phoenix's most prominent individuals! Only Almighty God could orchestrate that! Tossed aside, He had moved in with an elaborate plan of rescue. All because He deeply loves the orphan!

Over the years since Ruby came home, her progress continues to astound all who saw that first picture of her, heard the early reports that she "would never do anything" or have seen her MRI. She is a thriving miracle and all credit goes to Almighty God, the maker of heaven and earth.

It is our joy and privilege to be Ruby's mommy and daddy. We couldn't imagine a more valuable treasure to be gifted with, and at our age! We regularly comment to each other how difficult it is to fathom how much of the world does not grasp the privilege of adoption nor do most realize what is missed by not embracing special needs treasures.

From our vantage point, each home needs a Ruby and we are completely convinced that the world would surely be a kinder and gentler place if each family were gifted this joy.

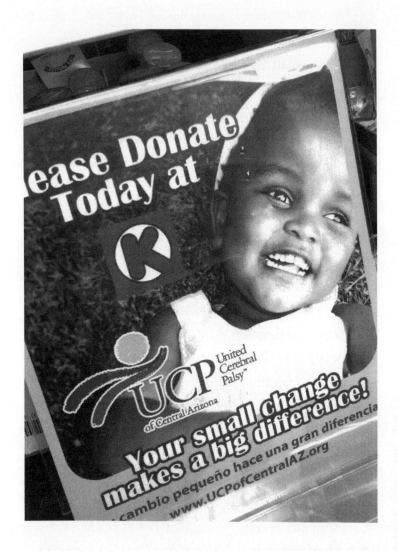

Ruby's face appears throughout many of the Circle K stores in the Arizona area where shoppers are encouraged to place their change.

Every single day we relish the moments and joyfully share with anyone who will listen, Ruby's journey of rescue back from the grave. We don't take her life lightly. It's still fragile. It will always be fragile.

And we will always treasure every moment we have with this most precious gift.

And we are forever convinced that when doomsday medical professionals in Africa were declaring, "Forget her! Don't waste your time! She'll never do anything!"

Almighty God was booming from His holy heaven, *"Oh really? Now watch this!"*

Our Family

Graham & Savannah's Wedding - July 2014. Dwight & I with 11 of our 12 treasures and their families. Emma, the Founder and Director of TheGemFoundation.com (a home for special needs treasures) was unable to attend. We held up a framed print, so they could still be "with us." We have seven (so far) grand-treasures, three of whom are also adopted.

Easter 2015

Ruby pictured with her mom and dad and siblings that live at home...Nehemiah, Jubilee, Elizabeth, Liberty, Elijah, Dwight, Linny holding Ruby and Isaiah. Our family awaits another son, our 13ᵗʰ treasure. We have named him JonWesley. He waits in China and is also in a wheelchair. God's love for the orphan is lavish!

JOIN US:

Join a GO Team!!

You are invited to join my husband Dwight or I on a GO Team to go serve the Special Needs treasures in a developing nation of Africa. Trips are led four times a year: April, June, September and January.

Email: **Office@InternationalVoiceOfTheOrphan.com** for more information and to request an application.

Sponsor:

Join us in sponsoring a Gem at: TheGemFoundation.com The Gem Foundation (TGF) currently cares for 26 Special Needs Gems. The Gem Foundation was founded and directed by our daughter, Emma, who has devoted her life to caring for the most vulnerable of all orphans. TheGemFoundation.com

Feed and Care:

International Voice of the Orphan (IVO) is a 501c3 that Dwight and I began in 2011 in response to the vast needs we saw while leading mission teams. Our work is sharply focused and can be found at InternationalVoiceOfTheOrphan.com

Feed: Join IVO in feeding meals to orphans in Africa, vulnerable street children in Africa and the largely forgotten children of a leper colony in India. Since it's inception IVO has fed over 400,000 meals to these three groups of precious treasures.

Care: Join IVO in providing medical care to orphans & vulnerable children with families in developing countries as well as medical care for the Gems of The Gem Foundation.

To contact the author: aplacecalledsimplicity@yahoo.com

11734055R00139

Printed in Great Britain
by Amazon.co.uk, Ltd.,
Marston Gate.